Dennis Fairchild

HEALING HOMES

Feng Shui — Here & Now

Dennis Fairchild

HEALING HOMES

Feng Shui — Here & Now

WaveField Books
Post Office Box 1781
Birmingham Michigan
48012-1781

For
Claudia

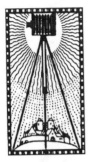

Fairchild, Dennis
    Healing Homes: *Feng Shui* — *Here & Now*

Bibliography: f.
Includes index.
1. Feng Shui I. Title
ISBN 0-9649981-0-6

© 1996 WaveField Books
Post Office Box 1781
Birmingham MI 48012-1781
e-mail HealHome@aol.com

Published in the United States of America.

Thanks to Dover Publishing for use of their line drawings
and to the several celebrated authors whose quotations are
used throughout the text. Every effort was made to obtain
permission to use material in this book and to publish proper
acknowledgments. I regret any error or oversight.

Additional thanks to Claudia Adams, Susan Armstrong, buddy
Stefan Brink, Beaunice Brooks, Michael Barney, the folks at the
Birmingham Community House, dear friend-editor Hazel
Dawkins, Phyllis Disney, William Dufty, Mary and Terry
Fairchild, handwriting expert Ruth Holmes, Bob Longacre,
Teri McCormick-Knapp & family, Raymond Merriman,
Katherine Metz, Linda Newman, Dennis Schick, Tracy Pratt-
Savage, artist-author Kyo Takahashi, Robert Thibodeau, Angel
Thompson, March Walker, Lorie Weiss, Nancilee Wydra and
all my students and clientele who helped along the way.

Use clear judgement when applying the principles of Feng Shui.
Ask questions, seek other opinions, experiment and experience.

"The fundamental delusion of humanity is to suppose that I am
here and you are out there."
    Yasutani Rishi

HEALING HOMES
Feng Shui — Here & Now
Contents

Foreword: William Dufty
Introduction: *Homeboy*

"Yesterday is but a dream,
tomorow is but a vision.
But today well lived makes every
yesterday a dream of happiness and
every tomorrow a vision of hope.
Look well, therefore, to this day."
Sanskrit Proverb

Contents

*"If you want to know how
important you are to the world,
stick your finger in a pond
and pull it out.
Will the hole remain?"*
  Maya Angelou

" In the world there are different
and still more different people.
Sit and mix with everyone,
the way a boat joins the river."
  Tulsidas

"There is no duty we so much underestimate
as the duty of being happy."
    Robert Louis Stevenson

Once upon the TV tube, in the early seventies, my wife Gloria Swanson went into a trance and heard herself saying that the physicians of the future would be physicists: instead of footprints or fingerprints, one day, newborn babies would be measured and identified in terms of their unique individual, energetic frequencies.

Given the extraordinary reach of network TV, it was only days before a renowned Italian scientist tracked Swanson down to correct her time line. The future she had talked about was already here, he claimed. And he was a part of it. He called himself a biophysicist. And his experimental clinic in Rome was called Centro Europeo de Bio-Fisica Applicata.

In her Fifth Avenue library, Dottore Giovanni Dotto held Gloria spellbound until well after dawn. I was so staggered by Dotto, I eventually ended up donating my fifty-eight year living breathing body for experimental purposes at Centro Europeo.

To me, that little hyphen merging biology and physics meant that the avant garde of Western science had arrived at the point where Oriental wisdom begins: that man and the universe are *not* two.

I thought of my adventures at the Centro Europeo as a kind of Lend Lease. American research institutions recruit guinea pigs. I would be a U.S. pig in a vice versa lab.

Dotto interrupted my antipasto one afternoon in Italy with a command: "Andiamo! Grappolo cancro choistro!" My crude English translation which I will forever remember was "Cancer cluster in the cloister."

In his Ferarri, Dotto explained the summons while navigating traffic around the hills of Rome. His treatment of Pope Paul VI was no secret from the clerical coolies, nuns, seminarians and low-level priests who staffed the Vatican. Buzz connecting the Pope's recovery and Dotto's Vatican house calls up clandestine stairways had created a flood of sick clerics lining up at his Centro. Among them, nuns living in cloistered convents obeying a vow of silence who had to get special Papal permission to venture outside.

The first seventy-five year old cloistered nun who turned up with what is called rampaging leukemia didn't ring any particular bells. But when a second elderly nun turned up with an identical diagnosis and identical cloistered address, Dotto reached for his Geiger counter, compass, binoculars, et al. Not to check up on the nuns. But their house. The convent. The cloister where they had been cooped up since Benito Mussolini was a young calf.

Dotto finally found a spot to park above the cloister. We took to the hills on foot, scrambling for a panoramic view.

"Ecco! Look," Dotto hollered, pointing to a copper-toned convent roof, gleaming in the late afternoon sun. The walls had been there for centuries. The copper roof looked brand new.

Now Dotto peered toward the beaches of Ostia through his high powered binoculars. Then he handed me the glasses and asked, "What do you see?" It was the radar towers of Rome's International Airport. Fiumicino.

The powerful radar beams from the airport towers swept directly across their copper roof. Day and night. Thousands of times every hour. Cooped up in that cloister, the sisters were cooked like ravioli in a microwave oven. The new roof had been a gift from American Catholics. It might cost billions of lire to undo. Dotto would have to begin the biophysical therapy on the Mother Superior.

The Greeks have no word for it. But Germans do: the untranslatable "schlimmbesserung." The closest anybody has come is "a so-called improvement which makes things worse."

The first treatises on Feng Shui in Latin are lodged somewhere in the Vatican Library in Rome. They were the work of Jesuit Missionaries who became dedicated translators and scholars of Chinese culture. They ran into the same trouble as Galileo and other stargazers; the four-hundred year misunderstanding this produced was only recently resolved.

1. Out of clutter, find simplicity.
2. From discord, find harmony.
3. In the middle of difficulty
   lies opportunity.
   Albert Einstein's
   three rules of work

The pursuit of happiness on the New American continent guaranteed rights aplenty to pale-faced people, but the Supreme Court upheld legislative acts of Oriental Exclusion — which not only kept out Asian immigrants but most of the culture of their continent. They were not repealed by our Congress until 1943, when Madame Chiang Kai Shek and the Generalissimo were our wartime Allies.

William Dufty, the prize-winning New York newspaperman, was drafted by General Hershey in 1942 and by Billie Holiday in 1955 as accompanist on her memoirs, Lady Sings The Blues.

John Lennon created a full-page cartoon mural for Rolling Stone celebrating the publication of Dufty's English version of an oriental classic, the legendary You Are All Sanpaku, in 1968.

Dufty's 1975 best-seller Sugar Blues has sold millions in many languages. He can be reached at WFD6@aol.com.

Even then, Madame Chiang couldn't help noticing that the Statue of Liberty in New York Harbor, hoisting her beacon to Europe's huddled masses, has her other cheeks turned toward the Pacific Rim.

After several centuries of piracy and plunder, we are all environmentalists. The ancient art of Feng Shui, revitalized and revamped by Dennis Fairchild, tells us what the Asians discovered aeons ago: environmentalism begins at home.

As a jack-of-all-intuitive trades who has amazed Motown's movers and shakers for over two decades, Fairchild has the jump on other friends of mine who retooled themselves as Feng Shui interns. He began as an entertainer. So his classes are entertainments. And so is this book. He just can't help it.

So read on.

William Dufty
Spring, 1996

As the end of our millennium approaches, the initiative is returning to where it lay a thousand years ago, on the shores of the Pacific.

Eastern influence on the way western scientists think...suggest that the world may be experiencing the reversal of the conventional direction of the flow of formative ideas. After two or three centuries of pummeling and kneading by western influences, the east is getting its intellectual revenge.

History has not stopped with a world culture made in the west. The sun has come up again on the other side of the world, and the cultural imperialism of the present and the future emanates from the depths of Asia and — increasingly and decisively, I believe — from the shores of the Pacific.

Millennium
A History of the Last Thousand Years
Felipe Fernandez-Armesto
Scribners, 1995

*"I am not young enough
to know everything."*
James M. Barrie

You came from Heaven
And I know your worth
You made a Heaven
For me right down here on Earth...
sung by Al Jolson

Introduction
Homeboy

The gospels proclaim it, and the songwriters second the notion: the Kingdom of Heaven is right here, on this planet. It's the only paradise we've got and we've screwed it up.

My seventy year-young mom in Florida lost twenty-five pounds in the year between Michigan visits. Granted, she had changed her menus. The thing that disturbed her most since last summer, she said, was insomnia. She was staying up later and later watching TV commercials every night.

平
和

The Chinese character, called a kanji, for "peace" resembles a tall home surrounded by trees.

After intense interrogation, I discovered that Wal-Mart had been hammering together a superstore behind her house during the past few months. Their floodlights invaded her bedroom, where we spend a third of our life, and glared directly onto the pillow where she rests her lovely Taurus head, making for night after sleepless night.

The Japanese, Chinese, Aborigine, Eastern and American Indians — some of the world's oldest and most spiritual cultures — believe that every rock can breathe. Not just plants but your home. We need overhead roofs, walls and floors to protect us, windows and doors to provide light and inspiration. Our homes are more than an address: they are directly hooked to our life. A person and their habitat are not *two*.

Places are reference points for individuality and more than a zip code or reruns of *This Old House*. They define who and what we are: "I'm an Eastsider," "a Midwesterner." Everything has an effect on us: the color of house, the drive and sidewalk. Many global cultures believe that everything is "alive" and vibrating in variable frequencies with personal energies.

Have you ever screamed at your car when it wouldn't start or warm up quickly? Or walked into an empty apartment and greeted the walls with, "Hi, honey. I'm home?"

Ever whispered sweet somethings to your plants? Pets? Dreaded visiting certain friends because of the street where they live? Or had the creeps in their condo? We view our surroundings with a personal lens and can direct our own movies.

Usually, in most Asian philosophy, everything has an impact. Landscapes and furnishings. Neighbors and their German Shepherds or calico kitties. The dying tree next door looming over your driveway. Telephone and electrical wires above the garage.

Feng Shui (pronounced *fung schway*) is the ancient Asian belief that space and placement of things carry force, either favorable or not. Colors and shapes, location and where you toss furniture can either add to your strength or drain it away.

Think about a home you really loved. Was it the locale? The beautiful trees? Its high ceilings? Tall windows? Deluxe view? Whatever. Chances are, they reflect the principles of Feng Shui. Although Feng Shui illuminates 4,000 years of international, multicultural history, many, like my mom, sometimes think of it as a Chinese menu item. By definition, Feng Shui assesses how light, color, architecture, geology and astrology combine with surroundings to affect us where we live and work.

調
和

The kanji (Japanese writing) for "harmony" is similiar to the word "peace" and incorporates a tall building and tree design.

Rather than call Century 21 Realtors, my mom ran to Kmart and bought a pair of thick curtains to assure a better night's sleep. Simple, good and real Feng Shui. She bought a wind chime to create counterpoint to the early morning percussion of the garbage men. My younger brother hung it in a window next to her bed. Tinkling melodic tones "sing" her asleep after *Matlock* reruns.

Living space is sacred. It's *yours*. For many, location, what a dwelling looks like and costs takes

precedence over its effect on the total well-being of those who live or work there. Holistic healing aims to meld the mind to the body and spirit. We control so little but we can buy and move furniture. Feng Shui endeavors to integrate personal life choices and patterns to your space. Please police your premises.

I grew up in the Michigan boondocks in an all-white suburban General Motors ghetto, spending lots of time with my grandma on Dollar Lake (a prosperous name for a nearby body of water). After high school, I landed at Michigan State University with an 80,000 population, a hundred times the neighbors I'd had. There I met my first Feng Shui guru: a tall, dark and handsome prince disguised as a student.

"The mountains, I become part of it...
The herbs, the fir tree, I become
  a part of it.
The morning mists, the clouds,
  the gathering waters,
I become part of it.
The wilderness, the dew drops,
  the pollen...
I become part of it."
  Navajo Chant

Alone in my dorm room with nothing on but my Hanes briefs and FM radio, there was a knock at the door. A *very* loud knock. It flew open with a crash, and there stood a six foot Asian stud in elegant bell-bottoms and sandals staring at me. He had a huge Gucci trunk in one hand, and a violin case and bonsai tree in the other. He glided in with the ease and command of an aikido master. Scanning the bare square room, he pointed to the twin mattresses against the window with folded sheets and towels on them.

He mimed astonishment, and shouted in staccato words, "Whose bed *that*? Mine?"

"Yours," I timidly replied.
He roared with laughter.

"Must move against wall," he decreed. "Now!" The last syllable pronounced with great affection still sounded like "now." It also turned out to be the diminutive of his name, Naohiro Yamada.

I hit the floor with my bare feet, responding to commands from this samurai decorator-from-hell. Then, our space was invaded by a platoon of Asiatic relatives and flunkies chattering in Japanese. They seemed to be critiquing the curtains, sneering at the furniture, rearranging the desks, scouting the closet space, giggling about the bathroom. Then they disappeared.

I was face-to-face with the first Japanese I had ever seen in person, off screen, up close. My only connection to the Orient was the high school graduation present from my parents: a 1968 Toyota, and a flashback to one of Dad's favorite World War II movies.

The placement of Nao's plant, the positioning of our space, everything had to conform with Feng Shui traditions and Japanese astrology to bring us luck.

A year later, I was hired as an actor (to sing and dance) and professional astrologer (to predict who couldn't) in the Broadway rock musical *Hair*. My summer dream job took me abroad visiting mystical locations like Stonehenge, Findhorn, Bali, the Bermuda Triangle, Delphi and the ancient pyramids. Not a shabby itinerary for a kid raised in the Michigan beanfields who had never even been across the water to Canada.

In the last lap of my contract when the fun of out-of-trunk living began to dissolve, I settled into an apartment outside Detroit and a new job as a talk radio host. After years of evening call-ins about other people's crises, I started saving up to apply for a home mortgage.

Then, my *real* Feng Shui experiments began.

"The man whose mind is rounded out to perfection Knows full well Truth is not cut in half And things do not exist apart from the mind."
Chan-Jan

Chapter One
Homework

Doctors use labels like overweight, diabetic and neurotic to describe specific human conditions. Victorian, Oriental, Sophisticated or English Country is interior designer vernacular. Feng Shui has its own lingo too.

Some people walk with their head held high, chin up, chest out and move confidently. Others gingerly shuffle along with glazed eyes, drooped shoulders. New, shiny cars have a different aura than a noisy, rusted-out heap. Ditto with newborn babies and young puppies in comparison to great-grandma or the neighbor's twenty year old, ninety pound cat.

The "ch'i" kanji means energy, life.

Asians call energy "ch'i" (pronounced *chee*) and everything has it — people, pets, plants and places. Ch'i is either invigorating and virile or infertile, stale. Like filtered bottled water versus tap, Godiva chocolate or no-brand knock-offs. Quality, quantity. Eastern Indians call ch'i *prana* — breath. In Japanese, *ki* or *qi*, means life force. You say "poh-tay-toe," I say "attitude and ambiance." It's all the same. Just think of ch'i as energy.

Which do you think has more ch'i:

• The Sahara Desert or Amazonian rainforest?
• A smiling or frowning face?
• Dried flowers or fresh?
• Your basement or CNN President Ted Turner's Atlanta penthouse?
• Fast-food takeout or a home-cooked Thanksgiving dinner?

Simply put: a rainforest, an effervescent smile, fresh and alive flowers, places aboveground and Aunt Maxine's fresh baked bread each possess more ch'i than their opposites.

Just as people become healthier when maintaining good eating and exercise habits, color, seating arrangement, furnishings, lighting, music and aromas either enhance or diminish a home's ambient energy, too. Repainting dirty walls, re-hanging doors that bang into one another and re-oiling squeaky hinges are just a few ch'i energy increasing examples.

The Yin Yang Thang

Yin and yang are the negative and positive principles of universal life. The colors represent the principles of light and darkness, male and female, hot and cold.

The world is filled with forces that press in on and affect us in many ways. Small is different than tall. Morning ain't night. High isn't low, happiness and sadness are not the same. Joy, sorrow. Up, down. Right, left. Love, hate. All are variations of a similar theme.

Each energy is unique and becomes more clear when you understand its opposite. Warm, for instance, means something more precise once you've been frozen. Quiet is appreciated more after experiencing loud. The best part of breaking up is when you're making up. Get the picture? One works off the other; everything changes into its opposite.

Yin and yang, the Asian concept, are differences and the mutually supportive dynamics of things and, in Feng Shui, places. Yin is expansive, dark, feminine, rounded, curvy, flowing.

Yang is concentrated, light, masculine, blunt, squarish, straight. Originally, yin meant "cloudy, overcast"; yang, "banners waving in the sun."

Dark, depressing corners brighten up when lit. Cluttered areas become spacious when organized. In balance with one another, they encourage happiness. Hospital rooms have more energy when filled with fresh flowers, vibrant smells. Clean windows provide more light; heavy curtains darken. Damp, mildewed basement smells interfere with enticing kitchen aromas.

Buckminister Fuller, daddy of the geodesic dome and other architectural wonders, said there is no right or wrong, only right and left. If something is too much one way, balance it with an opposing factor. Know thyself, know your place.

家相

"Ka-soh," the kanji for Japanese Feng Shui.

There are many schools of Feng Shui but all derive from a common source: making the space you occupy work for you, whether home or away.

Feng Shui philosophy originally revolved around grave-siting, called the Form School with its emphasis on location and terrain. In this system, good homes featured landscapes that embrace you like an armchair but protect like a pit-bull. Shapes and topography had extra special meaning. Genghis Khan, it's said, fell from glory soon after his mother's tomb was demolished by enemies.

The Compass School assigns specific qualities to every direction. Here, financial sectors are located in the southeastern areas of a home; the southwestern spots — with their subtle, gentle illumination — bring luck to lovers. In the Compass School, every nook and cranny of your personal space is unique.

The Black Hat Sect disregards precise compass direction while, nonetheless, using attributes of the Compass School, choosing instead to align everyone's home facing north. Some Feng Shui books use this particular methodology since many people don't know their right hand from the left, much less east from west. If this is you, get yourself a compass or find a Boy or Girl Scout.

Back when Feng Shui first began, folks were coping with monsoons not microwaves. There were no in-house toilets, no bidets — only holes in the ground for collecting "night soil." Compasses were also difficult to find.

Feudal Japan had the most detailed sumptuary laws in history: what homes should be like, who to live and dine with, where to sit, what to wear. As twenty-first century residents, we can learn from all three streams: take from the old and make it new. Use what works for you. Honor the past, but acknowledge and embrace what is current.

This book aims to de-mystify the ancient arcane into modern mellow.

Chapter Two
Homebase

One of the first Feng Shui tips before acquiring a living space is to research the luck (or lack) of previous tenants. Ask 20 questions. How long did they live there? Did they prosper? Did anyone divorce or die in the place?

Like being belted into a Honda with a chain-smoker, a home's "smell" also rubs off on you, too: bad and good. The energies and ambiance of those who previously lived, laughed, cursed and complained in a home surrounds that of the next owner. I call it *residence inheritance*. Think "cooties." Remember the bloody walls in that infamous home in Amityville? Or Jack Nicholson's nightmare winter hideaway in *The Shining*?

Places possess "residence inheritance" carried over from previous tenants. Research the happiness of those who lived in the home before you and make it yours.

Not long ago, Paula, a young, single TV producer with long lashes and even longer legs, moved into a deluxe townhouse in an exclusive Boston suburb. The building was an architectural dream: tall ceilings, quiet, spacious, ten foot high windows and breathtaking views of nearby woods. Although rent was steep, the place (she thought) was perfect.

Unknown to her when she signed on the dotted line, the home's previous pair had filed Chapter 11, were unable to have children and divorced after ten abusive years. Months after moving in, Paula's life turned into a tumultuous three-ring circus, complete with clownish lovers, failed professional projects and unexpected high utility bills.

When her lease was up, she rented a new townhouse down the street within her price range. Shortly afterwards, she copped three Emmys, a better paying job, married a wealthy stockbroker and is now the happy mother of two.

America's romance with complexity and "bigger is better" doesn't cut it with Feng Shui. Thoreau said, "Most people are needlessly poor all their lives because they think they must have a house as their neighbors' have. Consider how slight a shelter is absolutely necessary."

Historic castles, conspicuous mansions and gaudy plantation homes were difficult enough to heat or cool, and hurried many titled tenants off to the poor house. Chinese author Li Liweng says, "The most important thing in a living home is not splendor but refinement; not elaborate decorations but novelty and elegance. Cherish the virtue of simplicity."

One of my primary goals for a new home was to find safe storage space for my computer files. For me, this place carried the right ambiance: tenants lived a healthy natural lifestyle and into their nineties, the husband was a successful banker, the son an award-winning journalist and author. And the number was 883. Addresses with 8's are considered positive, money magnet-like homes. Not only that, the street name was Gold, a metaphor for moolah.

The lawn had never OD'd on chemicals (good for innovative work), the paperboy could "hear" the dandelions and flowers growing (providing

"Lift the stone and you will find me; cleave the wood and I am there."
Jesus

abundant opportunity), plus it was surrounded by two hundred year old maple trees (bestowing wisdom from elders) housing several extended families of squirrels and other critters (terrific for attracting help from others). The neighborhood also has a waterfall (another natural money magnet) and no industrial buildings, factories or cemeteries for miles (assisting in peace of mind) . Within a year of sweet dreams, I was signed as a columnist for an international magazine and began a lucrative speaking career. Superstition? Mondo deco or good Feng Shui?

Living on or near water is a plus, provided that the springs, lakes or streams are clean and flow rapidly. Stagnant water inhibits income. I can hear a nearby waterfall from my bedroom window all day long. The water quality in your home is vitally important as well. If your water is chemicalized or rancid, use the MasterCard to buy yourself a water filter or purifier. The better your drinking water, the better your potential for greater income and creativity.

Feng Shui suggests it is bad luck to move into a residence when pregnant because the unborn child may be restless and lack direction as an adult. Joleen, a thirty-ish CPA student of mine, was ecstatic with news that she was expecting

"The world is its own magic."
Shunryu Suzuki

13

her first baby after years of attempts. After discovering her joyous, long-awaited news, she and her GM executive husband moved three times before the baby was born. Today, James is a rebellious, unfocused teenage son, floating from one dead-end job to another. A victim of poor Feng Shui.

Before closing on your mortgage, check out the height of neighboring homes. It's unfavorable to live next door to a taller building that overshadows yours. After Taiwan's Bank of China opened in 1989, neighboring businesses and residents suffered diminished profits and blamed it on the towering monolith.

It's bad Feng Shui to live in the shadows of taller buildings.

"Bigger is better" applies to Feng Shui when your home is the tallest. When nearby buildings are higher than yours, aim a small convex mirror from every nearby window toward the offending area, or keep a wind chime or spinning mobile moving in your foyer or front entrance.

Chapter Three
Homestead

3

Does your front door need a fresh coat of paint? Or address numbers that shine? Is the front lawn green or ghastly?

Like a business card, your front entrance connects the outside world with your own. It's the "mouth" of your home, your public image. Its condition, color and maintenance empowers or diminishes the health and happiness of everyone who lives there. When a door creaks, the roof leaks or basement reeks you feel poorly, too. A well-kept home affects those who dwell there and makes waves in the neighborhood.

玄関

The kanji for "entrance."

The main entrance is an important place to begin auditing your space. It's the one originally designed for a home, whether you normally come in and out by a back door or garage, or take the back alley way into your apartment building. Ch'i energy gravitates to and enters your place from the front, so make a point to open your front door every day, even if only to fetch the mail or grab the newspaper.

Keep your sidewalk, driveway, doorway and welcome mat clean and uncluttered to invite opportunity, freedom from restriction. Slap fresh paint on the door every spring, lubricate all hinges regularly to invite opportunity, keep you active and mobile, and liberate you from outside restrictions. Windows, garages, walkways, doors and walls symbolize the eyes, mouth and limbs of residents. An unkempt, messy front porch or entry way is as attractive as an unbrushed, unflossed presidential candidate is to a baby.

Mend broken sidewalks to prevent neck or back problems and promote longevity. A good Feng Shui home has walk-ups or driveways that flow in a gentle curve rather than straight as an arrow. They disrupt the happiness of those they target and disturb creativity. Like a finger poking your eye. Stagger an odd number of flowering plants or bushes on both sides of straight walkways so, that when approaching the main entrance, eyes dart back and forth like spectators at Wimbledon.

Outdoor lighting, fountains, ponds or statues staggered in the same manner or a weather vane or pinwheels on the right and front side of the walkway as you approach the home also counteract this unhappy straight-way feature. Entrances without any sidewalk or a lead-up walkway are considered poor Feng Shui. Here again, outdoor lighting or zigzagging colorful plants are quick fixes.

Take a look at the "live green" in your front yard. In your back garden. From your bedroom window. Too many evergreen yews or weeping willows is thought to portend bankruptcy or marriage breakdown; an odd numbered (usually, three or five) cluster of trees and shrubs are best. Vistas obstructed by too much green beget arguments indoors. Naturally healthy, unchemicalized lawns, blooming flowers and spaces where birds feed and squirrels frolic portend good fortune. The more life on your lawn, the more life in your home.

Dying plants around the front door can erode the health of the elderly. If a shrub, tree or limb breaks, remove it pronto. Be sure to rake all dying leaves and fallen buds ASAP. Obstructed vistas beget arguments indoors.

Homes should not squat close to a main road, at a dead end or cul de sac. Glaring headlights cause restless sleep and arguments among bed partners. Living on straight avenues or speeding traffic superhighways has unfavorable effects. Happiness leaves as soon as it arrives. In the line of fire, the busyness and headlights act as bullets or missiles, penetrating your peace of mind. Try installing a fountain, a windmill, whirligig or weather vane. Or place round convex mirrors in windows pointing in the direction of the traffic and throw away the tranquilizers.

"Everything is holy!
everywhere is holy!"
Allen Ginsberg

車寄せ

The kanji for "driveway."

The driveway connects you to the main artery. An even, unbroken driveway contributes to health and well-being. Irregular, bumpy or pot-hole ridden ones are not good Feng Shui. Paving your driveway with mulched dirt or leaves from your yard may prevent circulatory hassles and arterial tension. Lining a drive with plants increases opportunities, provided they are well-tended to and not allowed to remain after the blooms fall. Evergreen shrubs, in small groups, are very auspicious.

Drives that are wide at the street and narrow near the garage suggest that money will quickly leave and financial opportunities shrink. Lighting your drive from the street attracts both good ch'i and prosperity. Circular drives in the front or back of a home disperses energy and makes dwellers restless. Fork-like driveways suggest ongoing quarrels, with family members choosing separate routes rather than acting as a domestic unit. Painting red-dotted lines or laying red-colored bricks in a diagonal dash-like pattern across the driveway can counteract this problem.

To increase wealth, status and social standing, the front door should be slightly elevated, never below ground level. If sunken, illuminate the porch, walkway and landscape with outdoor lighting or with spiralling, tall-standing shrubs. Keep large rocks away from main doors because their heaviness is said to increase divorce rates, dull enthusiasm and will diminish personal happiness.

Most homes in my neighborhood are at ground level with sodded front lawns and flat walkways shooting like an arrow up to the door.

After moving in, I built a small wavy hill and constructed a curving walkway made of round moon stones up to my front door. Just days after my freshly seeded hill began to grow around the new thirteen (representing the number of lunar "months" in a year) round walkway stones, I was hired to host a prime time radio talk show for a popular broadcasting station out of the blue.

In most cases, round shapes are better than square, straight ones or sharp angles. Round and curvy (yin) designs in a home suggest growth and happiness; straight sharp (yang) lines are considered static, angry and harsh. Circles symbolize a mother's breast and the sun. Circular prayer wheels are found in ancient Egypt, Tibet, Greece and Japan and imitate the rotary movement of the heavens. Rounded stained glass windows are common sights in churches. Straight lines are aggressive, like a child running with a sharp, pointy object. In most cases, when in doubt, go round.

The kanji for "view."

Surroundings influence us profoundly. Would you rather live next door to a factory or a garden? To prevent financial misery and unhappiness, traditional Feng Shui says the front of your building should never face a funeral parlor, graveyard, church, prison, police station or gambling establishment. If yours does, keep the window shades down or call a realtor! The secret of home and womb is one.

"If you cannot find the truth right where you are, where else do you expect to find it?"
Dogen

Doors and windows invite sunlight, air and friendship. In the same way vital information passes through our five senses, various styles and shapes of windows and doors determine the quality of ch'i for a home. Perceiving the world through prison bars is different than a view from a picture window.

Rounded entrances and windows enhance creativity. Square ones may exaggerate conservative, petty perspectives for residents. Hang flower boxes in square windows to increase objectivity and open-mindedness and bless each petal. Homes with ornate or gingerbread trims around front entrances make completing indoor projects difficult because of the melange of angles. Formal or minimum trim is best and brings focus and determination to dwellers.

Front doors need to be the largest in the house and always open inwards. To increase family unity and prevent domestic squabbles, make sure front double doors are the same height, color and material. Wooden front doors with a windowed upper half are good for private homes but are preferably avoided in apartments or duplexes — try all-wood ones instead.

Main entrance doors with prison-like security bars and those made entirely of glass or metal scare away healthy ch'i and gentlemen callers not just cat burglars. If neighborhood thievery is common, place a statue of a dog, lion or dragon in your foyer facing the main street or hallway to act as a protective "psychic guard dog."

Outer doors should open from the same side and line up exactly in order to invite opportunity and beneficial ch'i. If your porch door hangs on the left but the main door is on the right, feelings of disconnectedness and paranoia is increased.

"Ring the bells that still can ring.
Forget your perfect offering.
There is a crack in everything.
That's how the light gets in."
Leonard Cohen

In this case, paint the inner space in-between the front and screen doors black or red to correct this and prevent costly trips to your shrink. Solid doors in vestibules or mudrooms create a feeling of disharmony as well. Use windowed or half-glass ones, and keep all-wood doors downstairs open or remove them in summer.

"Dress" your home seasonally. Replace screen doors with glass storm ones when autumn arrives. Leaving on a screen door during cold weather is said to create fearful, rigid and inflexible behavior, and prevents help from arriving when needed. Change all burned-out front porch bulbs immediately and sweep the porch entryway and walkway daily.

"Home is the place where, when you have to go there, they have to take you in."
Robert Frost

Make sure that your home address or apartment number is well-lit and visible. Clear address numbers attract career and social opportunity.

Clothes make the man, it's said, and first impressions endure although appearances can be deceiving. The French perfected trompe l'oeil, pronounced *trump loy*, "fooling the eye," into an art form. The color of your front door sends a

Drives and sidewalks that are wider at the street and narrow near the garage and front entrance suggest diminished profits for residents.

certain signal, sometimes blending with the landscape, sometimes boldly standing out. White front doors say, "I will accept you as you are, please do the same in return." Neutral tans and beige, sepia white-brown blends project modesty and keeping up with the Joneses.

Another neutral color, brown, for a front door, transmits sobriety and an awareness of status quo. Like fair skies, blue evokes peace and constancy. Since the surrounding colors of nature always challenge a house, green doors seem to disappear into the landscape. Their hue suggests growth but is not favored for a front door.

In Imperial China, yellow was reserved for emperors or scholars who embodied wisdom and enlightenment. Yellow doors are at once cheerful and overpowering, suggesting activity. Red doors demand that one stop, look and listen; red is the color of passion, blood, ardor, Elizabeth Arden, fire and war.

For months, Richard, a professional jury-screener, and his partner were unsuccessful obtaining a loan for their bed and breakfast in Corktown. Days after painting its front door red, several banks phoned, tossing cash their way.

Wooden porches suggest a creative and sensitive space while cement ones urge others to keep their distance. My original front porch was a square-shaped, cement one — not the least bit inviting. It faced south, the career section of the home. My first stroke of perestroika was to get rid of its square columns and black wrought-iron hand rails.

The kanji for "Feng Shui" (above); the kanji for "light" (below).

"Do not seek to follow in the footsteps of the men of old; seek what they sought."
Basho

Last summer, I replaced its original concrete foundation with a wooden octagon (sending out protective *sha* arrows towards neighboring buildings), stained it silver (the color of metal coins, for prosperity) and capped off the tops of my round (creative-enhancing) columns. Feng Shui says this attracts financial opportunity and shuns obstacles from career paths. Forty-eight hours later, I got a call from a book publisher and signed a deal! Good luck or voodoo?

Front porch pillars need to be regularly scrubbed and painted. Decaying, paint-chipped ones invite short temper, breed prejudice and create relationship hassles. Round columns gently embrace those who live inside and act as tranquilizers, huggable prison bars that give you something to lean on. Squarish ones create tension because of their blunt sides. If your columns are sharp-edged or square, drape green ivy or a climbing plant around to take the edge off anxiety and entice positive ch'i.

But avoid hanging plants from front porch ceilings; keep them as close as possible to the ground. Hanging plants on a front porch say "I'm not sure what these homeowners want." Retire or recycle all plastic plant arrangements from the porch. They're tacky as well as toxic, and bees don't care for them either.

A recent *New York Times* story described how psychotherapists go about choosing their own therapists: from the decoration of another's offices! Plastic plants make them run for cover. Well-kept flowering or silk plants are a plus.

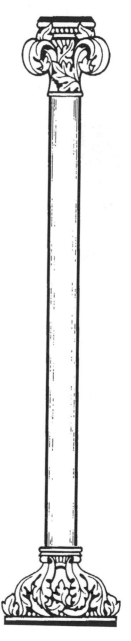

If you face a blank wall or section of one when entering the front door, a sense of isolation and confusion greets visitors. Hang a mirror or display a live plant or wall-hanging on the offensive blockade to create open space and invite friends, as well as helpful ch'i, into your space. It's also good Feng Shui to place a mirror on each side of the front hallway. Like walking through an airport metal detector, its mystical scanning "blesses" those coming and going and insures a pleasant visit.

Coat closets at the front entrance should be clean and roomy, containing only seasonal items. Storing winter boots in a front closet throughout the summer is a no-no, inhibiting economic change and creating arguments among family members. Keep umbrellas discreetly out of sight for this same reason. Closets, although hidden from visitor's eyes, have an impact on those who live at your address. Treat them like your bedroom: make them organized and practical.

Every object we see shapes space in some manner and has a subliminal effect. Our surroundings define us and everyone who lives there and how we relate to others.

押入

The kanji for "closet."

"It is only with the heart that one can see rightly; what is essential is invisible to the eye."
De Saint-Exupery

Chapter Four
Homecoming

4

Shades of Scarlett O'Hara! The main entrance to Jo Anne's $950,000 Grosse Pointe home was just that: *gross*. Her extravagant, towering white and gold gilded stairway leading to the front door's main hall would have intimidated Rhett Butler.

Main halls and foyers are an introduction to your personal space. They're the first and last spaces you pass through and are very important. Making them warm, welcome and good looking is a "must." Eastern Feng Shui associates the foyer with the throat and how you relate to those entering the front door.

"In a hole in the ground there lived a hobbit. Not a nasty, dirty, wet hole ... nor yet a dry, bare, sandy hole with nothing in it ... it was a hobbithole, and that means comfort."
J. R. Tolkien

For good, honest and precise conversation, keep this area well-lit, clean and orderly to assure that each of you hears what the other is trying to say. Delegate all boots, umbrellas and other paraphernalia to another space, and keep it uncluttered to promote integrity and united, honorable exchange.

Jo Anne's mammoth descending runway pointed directly to the doorway, making me feel confused not welcomed as I entered. I didn't know whether to stand at attention like a servant, or bow quietly like a dignitary or child. I felt insignificant and edgy walking into her place, unlike a Feng Shui professional hired to do a job.

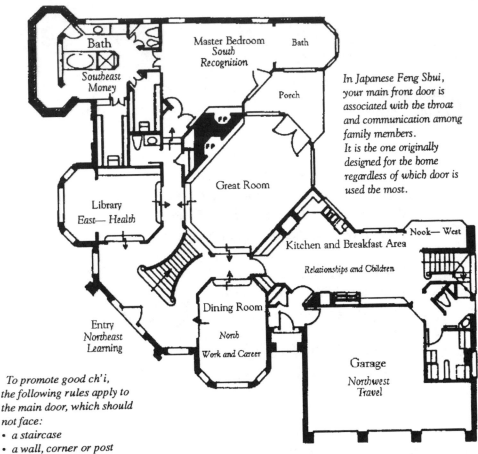

Bath

Southeast
Money

Master Bedroom
South
Recognition

Bath

Porch

Library

East— Health

Great Room

Nook— West

Kitchen and Breakfast Area

Relationships and Children

Entry
Northeast
Learning

Dining Room

North

Work and Career

Garage

Northwest
Travel

In Japanese Feng Shui, your main front door is associated with the throat and communication among family members.
It is the one originally designed for the home regardless of which door is used the most.

To promote good ch'i, the following rules apply to the main door, which should not face:
- *a staircase*
- *a wall, corner or post*
- *a back door or exit*
- *a wash basin, toilet or bedroom*

I told this wealthy auburn-haired sixty-some matron that this old house had one major problem. Everyone entering the front door feels an instant need to run to a private place, like her kids did every day, rather than gather for coffee-talk in the kitchen. It's common in many homes designed like this one. And there *are* solutions.

Staircases leading to upper stories and directly facing a main foyer or front door are a major Feng Shui no-no. Visitors will feel uncomfortable and want to escape to the nearest exit.

Jo Anne acknowledged that everyone in her house did their own thing. Her spouse and kids all went their separate ways, ate meals solo at different hours and rarely spent time together as a family. Ditto if you live in a split-level and have to climb up or down stairs to get to main gathering rooms: folks don't know what to do or where to go! In Jo Anne's home, family communication was nil.

I suggested placing a small table with a music box or cut flowers to the side at the bottom of the stairs to take the emphasis off that grand staircase, another one at the top landing with an octagonal mirror on the wall behind. This, I thought, might relax traffic, making them want to hang out downstairs. And different-colored carpets from the main foyer targeting the living area or kitchen. This way, spouse and kids might want to gather and talk instead of flying upstairs to their private cocoons.

"I am missing the doorknob gene, the one that helps you identify tacky doorknobs that need replacing. It's the same DNA strand that provides insight into window treatments, light fixtures and trompe l'oeil. Maybe that's why I always found Martha Stewart so scary, like Big Nurse with a pastry bag."
Maureen Dowd
New York Times 1995

You're more likely to stop talking to the TV set and not eat alone when the foyer carpet is a different color or pattern from the staircase. Round carpets turn into "you are here" signs at the mall. Aim different color floor carpets to rooms on either side of the stairs to direct traffic flow and direct energy to other areas.

Jo Anne's back and front entrances were big Feng Shui problems. Walking in the front, you could easily see her rear door. To promote communication and good health, no two doors should be in a direct line with one another: the old "in one ear and out the other" analogy.

Here, home ch'i energy strolls in one door but quickly flies through the opposite, depleting both the vitality of residents and creating potential physical communication and health problems.

If this is your situation, place a wooden table with either a statue, clock or books on the top, or hang chimes, a beaded curtain or mobile in-between offending doorways. Pleasant objects that distract the eye may curb the impulse to escape, hide, move.

Walking through Helen's front door, a trendy Bloomfield Hills art gallery owner, I was immediately greeted by a blank wall and two hallways leading in opposite directions. *Not* a good Feng Shui "howdy do."

With my defensive mechanisms kicking in facing this cul de sac, I could only wonder *where* am I supposed to go?

If you face a wall or barrier when coming in a front door, angle carpets directing people where to tread. Embellish the space with art objects, paintings, wall hangings or other decorative items to make wandering eyes feel more comfortable.

Place plants here. Hang a wind chime. Arrange trophies, certificates or awards in south or north entries, the career and fame sectors for rooms, to enhance career potential and bring acknowledgment from peers. Stagger gold (like silver, the color of wealth and energy) framed recent photos of children in all western and eastern entrances to inspire your offspring to try harder and ponder their future.

"Believe that life is worth living, and your belief will help create the fact."
William James

Helen didn't accept a single suggestion. She wouldn't change a thing. Fixed and very set in her ways; she remains a recluse, although a rich one.

Like traffic cops, main hallways regulate speed and flow. They should never be dark, vacant or confining. Long, straight ones make one apprehensive, leery. Think of school and hospital corridors. Paint halls with bright tones and open them up with good lighting or reflective surfaces to invite spontaneity and happiness. Filling them with clutter or impedimenta can drive you, and company, crazy.

"Though we travel the world over to find the beautiful, we must carry it with us or we find it not."
Ralph Waldo Emerson

Walking into one of my neighbor's home was like strolling through a funeral parlor portrait gallery. Tintypes of long-deceased forgotten ancestors, framed flea market postcards of others long lost. Keep paintings and pix of deceased relatives, friends and other folks far from main entries. Hang them either in libraries or studies, or in the northwestern corners of your home, the helpful people sector for those who may assist you in the future. But not the front door!

Make your space inviting, melodic, healing and comfortable for all who come calling or courting. And hide bills and financial statements from entrances to prevent worrying about tomorrow!

What you *see* impacts how you *be*.

Chapter Five
5 *Homegrown*

"...If you are close to the Earth, you are close to people.... What an African woman nurtures in the soil will eventually feed her family.

Likewise, what she nurtures in her relations will ultimately nurture her community."

Terry Tempest Williams
Refuge

The magical qualities of earth and flowers are rich with history. The term "poet laureate" comes from the Roman custom of crowning poets with laurel leaves. Shakespeare's Ophelia in *Hamlet* proclaimed "pansies for thought." Cleopatra paid gold to have the room where she would welcome Mark Antony in rose petals two feet high, symbolic of love and a woman's beauty.

Feng Shui assigns particular flora and fauna with either magnetic or repulsive powers. A proper Feng Shui garden never resembles a southern California pet cemetery. Red plants are said to enhance energy and health; yellow buds enhance clear thinking and intelligence; white for purity; green fauna serves as protectors and brings fortitude; dark-colored flowers act as grounding influences.

Fragrant flowers pack more power than their decorative relatives. Keep plants clean of dead buds and leaves, recycling them in the compost pile. The south portion of a garden plot concerns itself with your rank, fame and personal power; the southeast with money; good health is assigned to the east; the northeast with learning; career influences live in the north; for help from others and luck when travelling, activate the northwest part of the garden; west deals with children and pets; a healthy love relationship is assigned the southwest.

In 1986 when I began my first compost pile, the average Chinese soil garden was producing far more food per acre than the modern American farm. Back then, U.S. Secretary of Agriculture Bob Bergland admitted that the Chinese fed their huge population by producing nine times more food per acre than the American farm using chemicals and heavy machinery. The Asian approach to agriculture is founded upon the golden rule of organic gardening, providing continuous crops for five thousand years in many areas.

"An oak and a reed were arguing about their strength. When a strong wind came up, the reed avoided being uprooted by bending and leaning with the gusts of wind. But the oak stood firm and was torn up by the roots."
Aesop

A garden should reflect nature. Although constructed by human hands, it should appear shaped by Heaven and not a cookie-cutter "landscape" designed by the township's computer.

In a way, trees were the first temples. Think of their shapes. How their branches reach to the sky. How the roots spread out beneath the ground like huge spindles, connecting the energy between heaven and earth. The Druids saw this. So did the Greeks. Worship your yard's deep-rooted survivors. And plant one for future generations.

Trees should be located far enough from sidewalks and drives to allow their roots plenty of breathing space, just like people. Our ancestors' earliest environments consisted of forests, animals and mountains. In our brief human lives, trees seem immortal, particularly evergreens which seem to never change.

Healthy trees act as our "protectors"; dying trees portend ill-health to residents, particularly the elderly.

Tree worship and forest folklore abounds in the early histories of many cultures. The Old Testament speaks of sacred groves and altars under oak trees. The Tree of Knowledge was front and center in the legends of the Garden of Eden in the Book of Genesis. Buddha received spiritual illumination while meditating under the bodhi tree and was reputedly incarnated some forty-three times as a tree spirit. The image of trees as dwelling places of the gods appears in Persian and Indian mythology.

"The clearest way into the Universe is through a forest wilderness."
John Muir

Today, in many parts of rural America, a birch, fir or pine tree shelters newly built houses as a talisman for a happy marriage. Near bridges, dams or other large construction sites, they can help avert disaster. Trees such as bay laurel, elm, holly and olive around a new home are said to protect places from lightning.

Your landscape should be carefully edited to showcase the natural beauty of local plants. Refrain from filling the front lawn with flora and fauna alien to your region. In Feng Shui, less is more; simplicity is sublime.

Home sites with an odd number of trees are greatly favored, particularly nut-bearers and evergreens. Oaks attract health and inner-fortitude; the birch breeds openness and clear-thinking. The walnut provides protection from outside forces, allowing you to follow your path more freely. Pine assist in meeting obligations and protect against feelings of blame or self-guilt. The elm helps combat over-idealism and stress.

The evergreen yew has an ancient reputation for immortality and protection. As a symbol of the Resurrection, yew was used on Palm Sunday Eastertide church ceremonies. It was considered unlucky, however, to bring it into a house, and it was never used for Christmas decor. Planted in churchyards and cemeteries to shelter spirits of the buried dead, a symbol of life after death, mourners at funerals carried yew branches which they dropped in the grave.

Ancient history binds the willow with weeping and sadness. Traditional emblem of grief and melancholy, the willow is also a symbol of forsaken love. Shakespeare's Desdemona sings of a jilted girl, "...willow must be my garland." Unkind souls send willow garlands to unlucky lovers dumped by unfaithful ones. Because it grows in wet places, willow was believed to cure rheumatism, which can flare up in dampness. Nineteenth-century science investigated this remedy and found it contained salicylic acid, the current treatment of... you guessed it...rheumatism.

In many parts of China today, they still cover coffins with willow boughs. The Irish consider the willow magical, capable of averting illness and harm and herald it as one of the seven noble trees of the land. They still use it as a charm to ward off enchantment and the evil eye.

"Perhaps nature is our best assurance of immortality."
Eleanor Roosevelt

34

Broken tree branches felled by age or weather should be immediately carried away or chopped up for firewood or mulch, else poor health may drain the vitality of young and old. In autumn, rake leaves daily and compost regularly to insure prosperity.

Folk lore aside, large trees also guard against the elements and deflect the eye from offensive vistas, inviting good Feng Shui. Because butterflies and song birds celebrate a happy home, bird houses and water fountains are welcoming to wildlife. Weather vanes and whirligigs keep life-giving ch'i flowing, particularly in areas where the live green is lean.

Keep your garden colors simple and discriminating, not gaudy. Rainbow assortments are not favored in Feng Shui. Red plants enhance energy and health; yellow buds beget clear thinking and intelligence; white for purity; green fauna serve as protectors and bring fortitude; dark-colored flowers act as grounding influences.

"Hope is the thing with feathers that perches in the soul And sings the tune without the words And never stops at all."
Emily Dickinson

Reds, golds and orange are preferred floral hues. Decorative red flowers such as geraniums attract wealth but must be pruned daily. Red or white impatiens bespeak excessive concern for the status quo, and portend an active life with little downtime. Flowering plants with dead blooms affect the health of the elderly.

Fragrant flowers pack more power than those without scent. Keep plants clean from dead buds and leaves, recycling them in the compost pile. The southern section of a garden plot concerns itself with rank, fame and personal power;

the southeast with money; good health is assigned to the east; the northeast with learning; career influences live in the north; for help from others and luck when travelling, activate the northwest part of the garden; west deals with children and pets; a healthy love relationship is assigned the southwest.

A garden lush with cornflowers is said to help establish balance in your love, family and work relationships. Add clusters of these pale blue flowering plants to the southwest and northwest parts of the garden to bring peace and harmony to your support system.

The daffodil, or chalice flower, is said to attract communications and politeness to a household, especially when planted in the garden's northeast section. However, too many of these yellow flowers is said to scatter resident's energy and focus. These are best used as an accent in your garden beds, preferably in odd numbers to insure open-mindedness and healthy discussions in the homes they surround.

The common but potent dandelion, named for the jagged leaves' resemblance to lions' teeth, is governed by the sun (the symbol of life) and is also called the priest's crown. Because its flowers open around 5 A.M. daily and shutter at 8 P.M., they served as sundials to shepherds to leave their herds and head home for repose. Feng Shui lore consider them beneficial. Home front lawns lush with these golden waving wildflowers are said to protect family members from calamity and poor health. Cancel the ChemLawn exterminator and toss a healthy dandelion green salad today!

The day lily signifies coquetry because its fragile flower seldom lasts a second day. Keep them at a minimum in your Feng Shui garden and immediately remove wilted blooms to insure good health. However, if tortured by dental troubles, root canals or mouth disorders, hold the Darvon and place a bouquet of day lilies on your night stand to help alleviate pain and toothaches.

The forget-me-not is traditionally used for grave sites and should be incorporated sparingly in home surroundings. Pull a forget-me-not sprig and recite the name of a loved one; it's said you'll immediately win a place in their heart. Weave a few of these delicate blue plants in the southwest garden corner.

Ferns, a favorite in yuppie watering holes, are considered auspicious, having the legendary power to bring good luck and confer wealth. Let this lacy live green luxuriate in the southeast and northern portions of your home to attract financial opportunity and soothe insecurities.

Race to the nursery and grab the hoe: no Feng Shui garden can have too many ferns!

Potted on both sides of the front and rear doorways, red geraniums are said to attract extra income and prosperity. White ones bring peace of mind among dwellers. Because they can survive harsh weather, geraniums assist in combatting ongoing household hassles. In kitchen and dining areas, they assure that food will always be on the table. White geraniums should never dominate a front yard garden; keep the flower bed red.

"The bough which has been downward thrust by force of strength to bend its top to earth, so soon as the pressing hand is gone, looks up again striaght to the sky above."
Boethius

The shiny green holly planted around a house or field is believed to repel evil influences. Folklore says that elves and fairies are attracted to holly. Medieval monks called it the Holy Tree: its spines represent the crown of thorns, the white flowers purity, the red berries the blood of Christ, the bitter bark, the passion.

"Nature, the Gentlest Mother, is impatient of no child."
Emily Dickinson

Legend has the holly first sprouting under the footsteps of Christ. Plant holly in your north or southern parts of the garden to attract prosperity and encourage a bountiful income.

The hollyhock has been long revered by Japanese Feng Shui for its beauty and the varied colors of its upward spiraling flowers. It's best used against walls or in garden corners. Young couples panting for parenthood should plant them (preferably red and orange) in the west and southwest sectors of a plot to promote fertility and enhance the embryological education of budding geniuses.

White lilacs are said to create disturbing thoughts and impair judgment and should be used sparingly, and never near the home or bedroom windows. Purple and blue shades are best.

Because their flowers and fragrance are fickle, inconstant and fleeting, they are an emblem of youth. When you're stuck in old thought patterns, toss a bouquet of bluish lilacs on the dining table or in the den and open up your mind. These are the flowers for writers and artists. Throw them to the divas in your compost pile once their aroma fades or toss petals into a pot of boiling water on the stove as natural incense.

The proper Feng Shui home avoids featuring marigolds — best used as a garden accent. Combine these pungent yellow-orange flowers sparingly with white or pink roses or other colorful flowers in-between them to neutralize their reputation for grief and despair. Although yellow is the color usually associated with intelligence and learning, marigolds are the exception. Too many attract despondency, disorientation; never let them be visible from bedroom windows.

The helmet-shaped flowers and shield-like leaves of nasturtiums symbolize bullheadedness and ego. It's said that clusters of these scarlet and yellow flowers can create family disagreements, especially if planted in the southwest or northeast portion of the garden. Their Latin name means "nose-twister." Better to let the dandelions run riot rather than cultivate disagreeable nasturtium blossoms.

A rose by any other name would...you know. The rose is forever linked with female beauty. Aphrodite, the goddess of love, it's said, created the rose. As she ascended from the sea, the foaming drapery that covered her turned into white rose bushes as it fell to the ground.

White roses bestow the ability to cut through the thick of matters. An abundance of red roses is said to generate vanity and pettiness amongst homeowners and should be reserved for the south part of your lot, only. Too many of these scarlet beauties attract thorny disagreement. However, yellow roses act as magnets to attract intellectual discussions and objectivity among *Crossfire* and *Nightline* panelists.

"Take it away at once," stormed
the Princess, stamping her tiny
foot in its embroidered slipper.
"I hate real flowers;
their petals fall off and they die."
Hans Christian Anderson

The name tulip derives from the Turkish word tulband, a turban, because of its shape. In the Far East, it is the emblem of consuming love. Presenting a potential suitor with a red tulip means your heart is on fire. They are said to be special havens for fairies and elves, who sing their babies to sleep beneath them.

Red tulips symbolize love and devotion when planted in uneven formation; yellow or variegated varieties instill the courage to fight for those you love. The darker the flower, however, the less their attraction for harmony and peace. Plant tulips in the southwest or east parts of the garden for luck with love and family.

"I believe a work of grass is no less than the journey-work of the stars."
Walt Whitman

A realtor friend of mine told me a story of one family's front lawn that resembled a crazy quilt: European wildflowers in the west, bushy foreign grasses in the east, assorted flora from overseas scattered throughout. Months after planting this technicolor mess, the owners filed Chapter 11 and the house went through several buyers and spurred a number of divorces. Since rotor-tilling the flowers, its current successful two-income couple remain happily married.

The good Feng Shui lawn is free of pesticides, inviting frolicking neighborhood critters and providing underground havens for your squirrel's winter bounty. Grass should always be well-manicured with all dying brown spots immediately remedied. Today, organic fertilizers can be found at most neighborhood lawn and garden outlets. Conscious-gardening, recycling and mulching provides positive brownie points for cultivating happiness and loving relationships.

The magical qualities of rock gardens, stone and gravel is also a large part of Feng Shui, enhancing both your landscape as well as personal power. The shape and size of granite objects inspire awe and have been objects of worship in many cultures. For centuries, stones have been cherished from Africa to Thessaly as "houses of God."

Greeks placed rocks on roadways in homage to Hermes, lord of communication, in order to sweep away the traveller's weariness and assure a pleasant journey. Celts strew horizontal and upright stones at Stonehenge as both calender markers and, some say, an airport for UFOes. The original idea of placing a tombstone above a grave was to assure that dearly beloved one's spirit might inhabit the stone.

Great stones were thought to be dwelling places for deities. The Irish Blarney Stone confers eloquence on those who kiss it. The Black Stone of Islam in the Kaaba at Mecca, a meteorite, is proclaimed sacred for it fell from the sky and landed in their holy place. Collect rocks and stones from prosperous neighborhood places rather than impersonal outlets.

American legend propose hanging a stone from the yard of a fertile family over the bed of wannabe mothers to beget healthy children. Similarly, hang round black or white pebbles from a nearby beach lush with ocean life over the bed of an expectant woman to provide easy childbirth.

One of history's most famous rock gardens belonged to the Hsi-tsung Emperor of A.D. 1100. When he ascended the throne, he had no sons, a state of affairs which Feng Shui advisors

"Fa-yen, a Chinese Zen teacher, overheard four monks arguing about subjectivity and objectivity. He joined them and said: 'There is a big stone. Do you consider it to be inside or outside your mind?' One of the monks replied: 'From the Buddhist viewpoint everything is an objectification of mind, so I would say that the stone is inside my mind.' 'Your head must feel very heavy,' observed Fa-yen, 'if you are carrying around a stone like that in your mind.'"
Zen Parable

attributed to the flatness of the surrounding terrain. As a result, he ordered that a mountain be built to the northeast of the capital.

Carts containing tons of huge rocks, water-worn into fantastic shapes, were brought from Lake T'ai near Sanchou, China's Garden City. The emperor had his sons but, due to his extravagance, he lost power. Again, less is more.

Home Improvement
Decks & Pools

Back porches and decks are an extension of a home and link your space to surrounding landscapes. Straight forward, unfussy furniture works best here and won't detract from Ma Nature's trees, grass and flowers. In outdoor areas, aim for solid wood or plasticized sitting arrangements. Keep the area clean and orderly.

Naturally weathered timber in light shades rather than colorful tinted hues are favorite Feng Shui choices for decks. Silvery birch or natural redwood tones are said to attract wealth and financial security. Decks and gardens close to the house should architecturally link the building to the outdoors. When farther away, use shrubs or tall grasses to create a soft background, giving the impression of greater space and to provoke new avenues of happiness and peace of mind.

A swimming pool should always be filled with water, even during winter. Empty pools turn into gaping black holes that wash prosperity and profits down the drain. When not in use, cover the pool and plant red flowering bushes or other colorful flora around all four sides to attract future financial

"Wisdom is like a clear cool pool — it can be entered from any side."
Nagarjuna

opportunity. To avoid financial mistakes, don't drain water into the septic tank or have outlet drains at both the shallow and deep ends.

Pools should not be located on a hill or on an elevated area behind the home. Keep it on an even plateau with the back yard for good luck. Pools with many corners or odd-cut tiles are not favored, they bring discontent among adults. Rounded and kidney shapes enhance family communication. To avoid arguments and domestic dissension, stay away from L- or U-shaped pools.

Remember: water is the element of life and money-making. We can live without food for days. But not without water. Watch your water and your income will soar.

"Do not divert your love
from visible things.
But go on loving what is good,
simple and ordinary;
animals and things and flowers,
and keep the balance true."
    Rilke

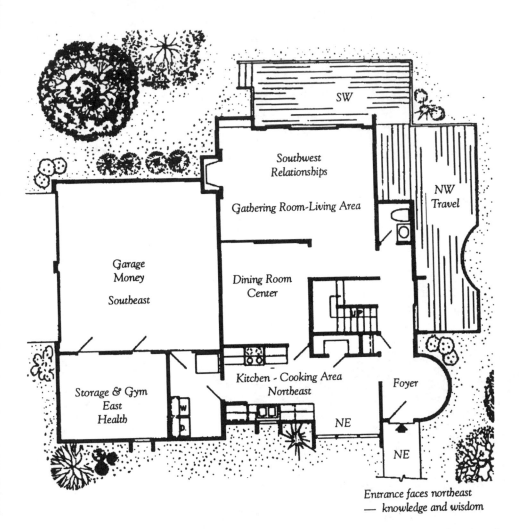

SW

Southwest
Relationships

Gathering Room-Living Area

NW
Travel

Garage
Money

Southeast

Dining Room
Center

Storage & Gym
East
Health

Kitchen - Cooking Area
Northeast

Foyer

NE

NE

*Entrance faces northeast
— knowledge and wisdom*

宿
命

The kanji for "karma."

When buying a lot to build a home from the ground up, consider the following about elevations and depressions of the terrain:

High eastern elevation: families will progress slowly but steadily; *low eastern depressions:* activity is large but rewards come and go swiftly, don't remain

High western elevation: occupants may suffer constant illnesses; *western low depressions:* intellectual stimulation is high and mighty; good for students, professors, writers

High western elevations: cooperation amongst residents; *low western depressions:* little regard for family, independence accented

High northern elevations: will acquire many friends, good social opportunities; *low northern depressions:* money will be spent easily, lack of financial awareness

Chapter Six
Homey

6

Color symbolism differs from country to country, century to century. Everything about color is never black or white. All colors are not created equal. For instance, white, while analogous to purity, innocence, modesty and peace, is also the color of weakness, infirmity and cowardice.

There's a world of difference between a red-breasted robin and a red bus. The New York City Art Commission recently fell flat on their collective faces trying to paint the city's bridges in designer colors. Some people surround themselves with colors that contrast with their personality while others demand a similarity and complimentary tones.

Social psychologists claim color helps manic depressives. Dark colors make them moodier. Bubble gum-pink walls in a prison, it's said, curb violence and physical assault. Spaces have composition just as paintings do. Color influences us.

"Our own life is the instrument with which we experiment with truth."
Thich Nhat Hanh

Although black is the color of mourning in the west and most of Europe, the flower of death remains a white lily. The black trappings of Good Friday are replaced with white, symbolizing Christ's resurrection, every Easter Sunday. The Devil's legions wear black; angels and the righteous robe themselves in white. Black and white knights do battle in legends as well as chessboards. White magic is associated with the good magician, black with its evil counterpart.

In Christian symbolism, angels, Jesus after the Resurrection, and Heaven's righteous dead are all commonly depicted wearing white robes. Processions of newly baptized worshippers, clothed in white, gave Whit Sunday its present name. Brides are clothed in white as a mark of virginity. Ancient Troy's Vestal virgins who tended the sacred fire brought to ancient Rome wore white to represent happiness and innocence.

During early nineteenth-century England, the hallmark of a Radical was a top white hat — the token color for impeccable moral and political principles. In many cultures, ghosts materialize in white wispy sheetlike forms. In Scotland, young children are given necklaces of white nuts in the belief that they will turn black when evil approaches. The Lone Ranger and other western good guys wore white hats when patrolling the prairies and bad guys wore black ones while waving the white flag of surrender. In America, fashion police frown on civilized folks wearing white pants or shoes after Labor Day.

Historically, while the white feather is a badge of cowardice and shame, white birds and animals are revered for their rarity: the white tiger is the

The Asian words Feng Shui translate to "wind and water."

Chinese king of beasts and American Indians honor the albino buffalo as sacred. Lewis Carroll's rabbit, who invited Alice into Wonderland's madness, was white too.

For centuries, traditional Feng Shui has discouraged us against painting rooms white because in Asia, mourners wear white uncolored muslin. Nowadays, white rugs and upholstery are signs that you're wealthy enough not to worry about soiling the furniture. Still, a home whose walls are totally white is still considered unlucky unless they feature a splash of silver or grey. "Marbling" is a wonderful remedy for white-walled spaces, especially when accented in rose or light blue tones, colors that stimulate life and love.

In contemporary Feng Shui, white walls are no longer feared or frowned on. The color mimics both the sun and moon and suggests inspiration or insight when tinted with another shade and used discriminately. Blue rooms are said to enhance emotional stability; purples or lilac for higher thought and objectivity. Browns and dark beige ones tend to "ground" a person in material, physical concerns and is best reserved for bathrooms or dens.

Although yellow is the color of the sun and relates to inspiration, intellect and economic gain (like gold), it is wise for jewelers to avoid using it in their home or business. The Chinese believe an aging man is similar to a yellow pearl implying that both diminish with time. In the West, yellow is often associated with cowardice; in the Far East varying shades of yellow-colored robes are symbolic of spiritual understanding and divine love.

"Every outer effect is the natural expression of an inner pattern. To battle only the outer effect or symptom is wasted energy and often increases the problem."
Louise Hay

Yellow is a recommended color for children's rooms and helps stimulate their mental skills. But never allow a yellow room to lose its lustre or sheen. Let your yellow shine like the sun!

The Latin, English, French and German words for "red" stem from a root word meaning "blood." In ancient times, when a victorious general rode in triumph through the streets of Rome, his face was painted red. Today, many cultures around the world associate red with passion, action, sexuality, bloodshed or force.

You're asking for trouble when you speed through a red traffic light. A red light district signals lust and passion just as the Bolshevik red flag once was a symbol of revolutionary ferment.

Sam, a timid accountant in his late fifties, recently redid his bachelor pad entirely in red: walls, carpets, fixtures, plates and tables. After his scarlet makeover, I was shocked to discover that after twenty-eight years at the same firm, he was suddenly fired because of the new angry, rebellious attitude he had begun to display. A "curse" from too much red?

"It is only shallow people who do not judge by appearances."
Oscar Wilde

Green is the color of nature, vegetation symbolizing growth and opportunity. Think of dollar bills. The "green, green grass of home." Green means growth. Life.

From Britain's Jack o' the Green, who wears emerald-colored boughs of ivy every May Day, to Peter Pan, green has a universal bond with fertility. In Feng Shui, seaside cottages and fish stores with green decor prosper because it is the color of live shrimp and crabs. But red is not advisable. It resembles cooked (make that "dead") seafood.

"You can only find truth with logic if you have already found truth without it."
G. K. Chesterton

I know of a man who was riddled with what is called "cancer." His recovery response was not good. Every wall of his home was painted green, not the color to surround yourself with when dealing with cells that multiply! Years after repainting his home and shuffling his furniture, this fellow has survived his oncological death sentence. Curiously, most American hospital corridors feature green walls and uniforms.

Specific shades and hues are good for certain rooms. What's your favorite color? What was the color of your childhood bedroom? Your first car?

Chapter Seven

7   *Homely*

Strategically placed mirrors bring the outdoors inside and are powerful tools in Feng Shui. They magnify light, enlarge claustrophobic spaces and deflect uninviting scenery or overstimulated energy that slams into you and yours.

Mirrors broaden and brighten long dark halls and tunnelling stairways. Rooms with odd or missing corners, as well as wings of U- or L-shaped houses, are easily restored by mirrors, illuminating empty, shadowy voids. Mirrors reflect heat, attract light to solar panels, refract unpleasant neighborhood scenery and make it easier to install your contact lenses.

Like Saturday night at a single's bar, a mirror's shape and size is important too. Keep away from using small mirrored-tiles because they're said to create emotional conflict. Generally, the bigger the mirror, the better.

Square and rectangular mirrors stabilize financial setbacks; circular or ovals are best reserved for sleeping areas to enhance intimate

"The cause is hidden, but the result is known."
Ovid

conversation and bring bliss between bed partners. Eight-sided mirrors, often used above fireplaces and in gathering rooms, unite the physical (square) and emotional (round) but use them discreetly.

Mario Cuomo's first decision as New York Governor was to remove the full length mirror inside the Albany mansion's master bathroom shower. Relegate all cracked, chipped, broken or scratched mirrors to your next garage sale. Not only are they tacky, they make you look worse for wear. Marbled and engraved designs diminish self-esteem. Leave fun house mirrors for the carnival midway.

The kanji for "dreams."

I remember Betty, a trim aspiring actress in her fifties, who displayed her vast collection of perfume and makeup on her mirrored vanity counter-top in the health sector of her home, the east. Always ready for her close-up, she sleeps in full make up with false eyelashes and gleaming fingernails.

"Looking good" is her thing. Telling Betty about her natural beauty and vitality falls on deaf ears. But one look at her homemade movie set explains it all: on every wall hangs a montage of marbled mirrors, looking like swirls of melting coffee ice cream on gaudy silver platters. Distorted reflections create surreal, problematic perceptions. How do *you* want others to see you?

To get the most miles from them, mirrors should be cleaned, dusted and polished regularly, like the family car. For friends in denial, wrap a yellow (the color of knowledge, intellect) ribbon around a mirror and give it to your pal as a gift, forcing them to look at themselves, saving them time and dollars on the therapist's couch.

"Think not because no man sees,
Such things will remain unseen."
Henry W. Longfellow

Make sure you see as much of your head as possible reflected in mirrors. Low-hung mirrors cutting you off at the hairline create tension, anxiety and a feeling you're not all there. Hanging them high helps elevate confidence and may prevent headaches as well as kinks in your back.

Years ago, I furnished my first office with large flowering plants and gifts from clients. One large, ornate gold-framed mirror in the waiting room continuously prompted nostalgic reveries from patrons like "that mirror makes me think about my grandma and when I was a small child."

I bought it at an estate sale from a sweet sixty-four year old Gemini lady with ten children who ran a day care center. I ignored Feng Shui philosophy. The vibes of previous reflections was affecting those who hurriedly arrived, checking their tie or makeup. (Imagine living in a home filled only with recycled mirrors from a department store dressing room!)

If you bring a secondhand mirror home, use it only as a backdrop for live plants or fresh flowers. Not loved ones.

Television cooking shows feature angled ceiling mirrors to allow cameras to see what's cooking. Kitchen stoves symbolize wealth because it takes money to keep food on the table. To increase your earnings, place a long mirror, aluminum foil or shiny metal behind the burners doubling their number. The more the kitchen stove burners, the more the food you can cook, therefore, the wealthier you must be! Use the same strategy to backdrop other success-orientated artifacts such as aquariums, desks.

The kanji for "mirror."

"Faith is the substance of things hoped for, the evidence of things not seen."
Hebrews 11:1

Susan, a struggling single mom with maxxed-out MasterCards, lives in a suburban bungalow. Short on cash to repair her broken stove, she dragged a hot plate upstairs from the basement. One morning, while waiting for her oatmeal to cool, she grabbed a silver serving tray — an anniversary present — from the kitchen cabinet to apply her foundation. After breakfast, her latest "makeup mirror" found a new home behind the hot plate since she couldn't afford to fix her Kenmore range then, just juggle bills.

The upshot: within weeks, a court order boosted her child support income and several lucrative free-lance gigs dropped into her lap. Now, after paying for the broken stove top from her extra earnings, the silver platter still lives in its own little niche behind the burners. And business is booming.

Mirrored high-rise buildings create a kind of drunken energy when walked past or seen from a moving car. If one of these reflecting monoliths face your place, plant a circle of trees or tall objects (like flag poles, bird houses, whirligigs) to transform your view and harmonize the chaos. Altering a vista is cheaper than moving and better for the nerves. But don't use mirrors to deflect tall shiny silver or gold buildings; this will only exaggerate frenzied pinball machinelike vibes and could tilt you out of control.

Tall buildings facing or overshadowing your abode can snuff out vitality and personal strength. Indoors, point a convex mirror at the towering culprits to reflect the offending building, making it appear smaller and shrinking negative vibes.

"Never be afraid of shadows. They simply mean there's a light shining somewhere."
Claudia Adams

Place a convex mirror at the rear of your home to "bounce back" noisy backyard neighbor barbecue drunks as well. Reserve concave mirrors for outdoors, and aim them at speeding traffic to slow vehicles down.

Look at your full-length reflection in a mirror every day. This allows you to see yourself as others do, revealing strengths and flaws. Schedule regular dialogue in front of a mirror: focus on seeing yourself clearly and totally, leaving vanity aside. Accept your very real and human limitations. Note how you feel framed by every reflected object in your space.

"There is nothing either good or bad, but thinking makes it so."
William Shakespeare

Chapter Eight
Homeopathy

Sound is a major contributor to stress. Noises: the neighbor's leaf-blower, rush-hour subway or the irritating whine from a dentist drill versus a Mozart lullaby prompt different responses. Positive, non-invasive sounds enhance well-being. Peace and quiet are major ambient influences for personal happiness and efficiency. Noise is disturbing because it both distracts and restricts.

"God respects me when I work, but He loves me when I sing."
Rabindranath Tagore

Quiet times in Manhattan apartments and condos are usually louder than Saturday nights in Manhattan, Montana (Yes, Virginia, there *is* a Manhattan in Montana, too)!

Sound, wind chimes, bells and music, is another Feng Shui province with which you can work to prevent over-stimulation or fatigue and bring harmony into your space.

The drone from towering high tension electrical wires, squealing car brakes or blaring boom-boxes make most people anxious. Feng Shui urges us to be our own musical arranger and orchestra conductor. Take the podium, grab the baton and whip dissonance into harmony! Let your CD player, radio or music box serenade you when noise gets offensive. Audio tapes featuring sounds of nature are soothing: natural music from oceans or waterfalls, bird songs or cooing children. If you're the chatty type try talk radio.

Hang glass wind chimes (a favorite Asian cure for spaces needing peace of mind) from the windows in all resting areas. Reserve brass or other metal models for hallways or backs of doors to announce visitors, alerting you to their arrival.

For centuries in China, shopkeepers used brass bells to protect them from theft. When hung in exterior doorways, they attract foot traffic and cash customers. At home, make sure your door bell works properly and has a pleasing tone. If not, find a cow bell or some chimes and a hammer, nail and string.

Before Barry Goldwater would unpack his senatorial impediment in his Washington, D.C., condo, he insisted that the doorbell chime out the Air Force anthem, *"Off we go into the wild blue yonder."* Imagine the Avon Lady's surprise!

Intermittent noise like ringing telephones, lawnmowers, screeching tires on pavement and screaming kids hamper motor skills, mental alertness and peace of mind. Take control of the volume knob on your TV. When the going gets rough, close the windows. Feed the birds and invite their melodies. Turn the volume down on your phone. Put on Tony Bennett or pipe in Muzak. Sing in the shower! Make your own music.

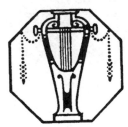

*"The silence
of nature
within
the power within.
The power
without."*
Gary Snyder

Chapter Nine
Home Economics

Sharks gotta swim and bats gotta fly. We all know about that. But sharks cruise the oceans in the daytime. Bats take flight without visible instruments at night. Some mammals hibernate through dark arctic winters. And some bipeds work their tail off through the long days of summer. Our built in biological clocks ticking away night and day are connected somehow to the way we shift behavioral gears.

"Getting wise" means, in the Ellington lyrics, beginning to see the light. Being "in the dark" is a metaphor for being out of the loop. Everyone is affected by light or its absence. Did you know that:

• Above the Arctic Circle, the sun sets around Thanksgiving and doesn't rise again until mid-February. Studies show that many Eskimo girls virtually stop menstruating during the dark winter unless purposely exposed to daily light.

• The New York Board of Education use bay windows and other natural light sources to increase students' attention and learning ability.

• Choreographer Martha Graham discovered that a high-powered spotlight enveloping her body, together with the roar of an expectant audience, brought instant relief from the agony of arthritis.

"Some things have to be believed to be seen."
Omar Muldoon

Light, mirrors, shiny metal objects and leaded crystals are important Feng Shui bandages for what ails you, especially if you're camping out in basements, dark attics or need a little illumination at the end of your tunnel.

I thought I was too early for a on-site housecall recently because the stairway leading to the second story chiropractor's office was pitch black. "Oh, it's always like this," replied the fifty-ish woman in white medical smock. How many patients have fallen down walking up these stairs, I wondered. And how could anyone possibly find this professional lady in the dark?

Patient flow was steady, she said, but walk-ins and new clients were nil. After replacing the stairwell with high wattage bulbs lighting up her name on the front marquee and office door as well as a few other changes in the reception and office areas, business began booming. "Let there be light."

Brighten southeastern walls and corners to attract financial opportunities. Rid rooms of dark shadowy corners to assure productivity. Illuminate entryways and hallways, making them comfortable to the eye and anyone walking barefoot to prevent toe-stubbing. Dim lighting increases uneasiness. Film Noir is all about that.

If you live below street level or inhabit a basement, refrain from using overhead lighting. Instead, go for table, floor or bucket lamps. They give the illusion that energy is rising rather than waning. You sleep less and rise earlier in a bedroom with an eastern window than one with western exposures. Credit that to extra light.

"Not to know is bad; not to wish to know is worse."
West African Proverb

Beware, too, of glaring light that makes you squint. Too much light is as bad as not enough. Lillian, an out-of-work Bloomfield Hills matron, lives in a U-shaped home with three glass walls facing east. Like being on a beach in Miami at high noon, hers is a home where guests need to wear sunglasses inside. Nervous, hyperactive and a definite candidate for Prozac, Lillian was a wreck.

If your space has too much light, fiddle with the windows. Louvers or venetian blinds (skip heavy curtains) allow you to control the right amount of radiance and give you power over the elements. Aiming outdoor lights at a U- or L-shaped home's vacant area symbolically recreates missing corners. The only dark empty spot in Lillian's home, you guessed it, was in the north: her career corner.

Be creative with light: wrap curtain rods with Christmas lights, toss colorful scarves over lamp shades, burn candles. For many, fluorescent lights cause everything from headaches to major mood swings and are not recommended. Full spectrum lights come closest to the natural qualities of sun light. You can find them on the shelves of most hardware or natural food stores.

"A map of the world that does not include Utopia is not worth glancing at."
Oscar Wilde

The kanji for "prism"
and "crystal."

Crystals, like prisms, create dancing rainbows when light catches them. Fine cut Austrian crystals are better than natural quartz; faceted is preferred over rounded. The clearer the crystal, the better. So polish all chandeliers!

Crystals look like diamonds but are cheaper on the MasterCard. They're pretty, they sparkle and they emit dancing rainbows when light hits them. Because of these traits, crystals symbolically bring energy to a space.

Hang one in your children's bedroom window to promote good sleep and prevent nightmares. Use them in windows facing unattractive scenery to "deflect" the offensive vista or in long hallways to "slow down the traffic."

For the best impact, hang your crystals from a red (the color of life and money) cord, string or ribbon in increments of 9 inches like 9, 18 or 27, according to Feng Shui folklore. Don't get frustrated if you don't have a ruler handy! Trust your instincts.

Smooth, round crystals provide a space with a relaxed, tranquilizing effect; multifaceted ones, due to their several cuts and more corners, deliver a more frenzied energy and are usually reserved for dark hallways or hanging in front of extruding corners. Have fun and be crafty!

Hang one over where you sleep to fend off financial reversals if your bed faces a bathroom door (and keep that door closed). Having trouble at the office? Situate a crystal on your desk targeting your personal rival. Toss away your

The kanji for "door."

styrofoam coffee cup and sip your Evian from a crystal goblet. Hang a small round one from your car mirror to prevent rush hour drive-crazies too.

Crystals are like vitamin supplements, they provide a degree of sustenance to what ails you but may not "cure" the problem. When you eat well, you need fewer mineral and vitamin pills. Crystals, like hugs, make things feel better. Still, you must take deliberate steps and make conscious decisions to obtain your goal and get what you need.

Cathy, a single social worker in her mid forties, filled every inch, window, corner and ceiling of her bed and bathroom with dazzling crystals hoping to attract a man. Rather than hanging her glass dazzlers in the southwest, her relationship sector, they were displayed in the east, illuminating health issues. No lover arrived, but she lost lots of weight. But now that she has new waistline and looks and feels better, a suitor is likely to follow. Flush those diet pills and shakes down the toilet, and try crystal consciousness!

"I'm astounded by people who want to 'know' the universe when it's hard enough to find your way around Chinatown."
Woody Allen

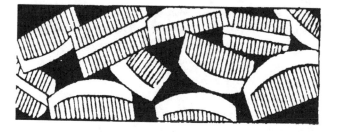

"For fast-acting relief, try slowing down."
Lily Tomlin

There are nine basic Feng Shui "cures" for promoting positive energy through a home or work place. Experiment!

• **Colors**: certain colors enhance life, others diminish. Black and red symbolize wealth and happiness. Brown and tan bring focus and "ground" a person; yellows and gold increase intellect and prosperity. Green is for growth, new opportunity; purple and light blues bring tranquility, spiritual awareness.

• **Bright Objects**: mirrors, reflective metallic items, crystals, prisms and shiny coins can lure ch'i to places that are ailing.

• **Living Things**: plants and flowers, live or silk (no plastic, please!) represent life and growth and circulate energy and opportunity. Plants in offices boost performance, productivity.

• **Sound**: wind chimes, musical instruments (real or photos of), pianos, CD players, tape recorders, stereos and chirping birds attract positive energy.

• **Moving Objects**: a fish tank of bubbling water, whiligigs, windsocks, mobiles and water fountains breathe new life into a space. Fill your "brainstorming room" with these!

• **Electronically Powered Things**: computers, TV sets, neon lights and microwave ovens encourage positive ch'i.

• **Heavy Objects**: statues, stones and other hard-to-move items prevent positive ch'i from leaving an area. Place these in southwest areas when relationships get rough.

• **Others**: red and black ribbons or tasselled fringe, bamboo flutes (symbolizing music) and bowls of fruit are auspicious.

Chapter Ten
Homeview

Many neighbors considered Manfred's family a bit mysterious and antisocial. He and his wife barely nodded to the people next door, and, even then, usually by chance in the supermarket checkout line at odd times of night. Their children occasionally disturbed neighbors but were never seen. Manfred usually mowed his lawn at sunrise while others were inhaling breakfast and quietly hauled his weekly trash to the curb for morning pickup the night before under a cover of darkness. Local gossip branded them urban vampires, lepers. Not at all. Only prisoners of an unhealthy Feng Shui swamp.

The family's home was an odd five-sided pentagon with corners and dormers jutting out every which way, and with only eight tiny windows the size of a Wheaties box. It's design was as bizarre as its inhabitants.

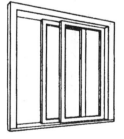

"Peek-a-boo! I see you!"
Mom's Worldwide

Windows, like doors, invite the nourishing influences of sunlight and air into our space. They connect our private lives to the outside world. People become clannish, withdrawn and more introspective when living and working in places with small windows. The world framed by a large picture window is very different from a shrimp boat porthole new like the tiny ones in Manfred's master bedroom.

His only bedroom window was the size of a soccer ball, which doesn't score any points in the game of Feng Shui love. Every window in the house had a dirty amber hue, like unbrushed teeth, not transparent or clear. Looking at the world through rose-colored glasses is one thing, but living in a home whose every window is tinted (particularly yellow) is a horse of a different color.

Living without natural light, your view of the outside world easily becomes jaundiced, tainted. Stained glass windows are good when used sparingly and in places where others meet and gather; the larger and more colorful, the better.

"More" doesn't always mean "merrier" when it concerns the inventory and size of windows. It's said that a house with an unusually large number windows (especially in a living room or bedroom) brings hassles with children and pets. Horizontal wooden blinds help cure this problem better than curtains.

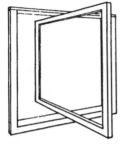

Windows that open at least 45 degrees and allow both light and air into a home are considered good Feng Shui, provided they accommodate screens to prevent insects or too much nature inside.

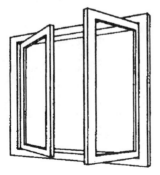

Older homes often feature tall windows that touch the ceiling. Elegant as they are, however, these often act as energy sieves, letting in winter drafts or allowing too much summer heat and sun inside. Unlike our great-parent's homes, today's windows have infinitely superior glazing techniques with no reciprocal energy loss or entry.

Windows are the Feng Shui "eyes" of a home. To insure the health of residents (and prevent wasteful energy bills), replace all cracked and broken windows pronto. While doing my own home improvements, I accidently cracked a kitchen window at eye-level and was very slow replacing it. During the time I lived with this jagged flaw, my behavioral optometrist hit me with a prescription and a bill for bifocals and a special contact lens. Not only that, my house-mate was discovered in need of cataract surgery. So save yourself eye doctor bills and routine eyeball liposuction and go fix your windows. While you're at it, give them all a cleaning!

What shape windows are in your bedroom, living area and kitchen? Wide or narrow? Are they hung high, inviting a panoramic view, or so low that you have to crouch? Do they open from top to bottom, side to side, or are they locked and sealed?

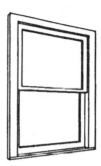

Windows are considered the "eyes" of a home. What shape and type windows dominate your space?

Windows rounded at the top that are arched or circular give off a soothing, calming energy, reminiscent of countless churches and other places of worship. Smooth shapes are considered relaxing, creative, inspiring and feminine, especially complimentary for bedroom hallways and gathering spaces. Square or rectangular windows which are wonderful for dining and work areas, fall into the practical "what's in it for me?" macho category. A gentle mix of each works best.

Skylights are glorious sources of light and energy. They invite the heavens into your home while providing natural illumination and peace of mind. They work best when discreetly used in cooking areas except above the stove top and in foyers or small, not long, hallways. For best results, avoid placing them above a bed or resting area, especially in children's rooms. In such situations, sleep will be more erratic and easily disturbed with someone or *something* watching over or falling on top of you.

To soothe irritability or boost self-esteem, the top of windows should be higher than the tallest resident. Rooms with a view should allow voyeurs to stand comfortably, taking in the scenery instead of stooping and craning the neck. Wide spacious windows support vitality, objectivity, and creativity, like a friendly greeting with open arms instead of an awkward hug that includes an armful of groceries. A place with many narrow windows signals apprehension, pettiness, like a limp, wimpy handshake. Give light space. Give your space light.

The ideal Feng Shui window opens outwards without disturbing anything in front or behind it, allowing you to breathe as comfortably as the home. Those that open inward encourage timidity, weakness. If this is your problem, place live plants like ferns and ivy or your stereo beneath them to help energize the area. Windows that tilt or French doors that open inwards are always going to be difficult to open when blinds are down or curtains drawn, making for frustration and anger.

You may have difficulty living up to your potential or give off false impressions if surrounded by windows that slide up and down but cannot open more than halfway. In this case, recycle all hanging curtains that puddle on the floor and treat windows with either brightly painted shutters, wooden shades or horizontal blinds. Glass or wood shelves enhance privacy and offer an excellent space to display live plants, crystals, awards or other energizing objects. Windows with a spectacular view should be treated like picture frames and, for good Feng Shui, painted a different color than walls to bring vitality and objectivity to residents.

Chapter Eleven
Home-Stretch

It's where the family *gathers* together. Remnants of the "hearth" may be reflected in the natural gas fireplace, but you don't cook or eat there, or bathe or sleep there. Unless you're a Liberace-wannabe, a piano might make it a parlor. It's a place where you receive guests, insurance peddlers, census enumerators, FBI agents. It's the most public space in the house, next to the foyer. In Feng Shui, it's what the heart is in the human body. It's front and center.

And whether you know it or not, everything about your living room: its color, decor, furnishings and their arrangement and location tells a visitor something about the status, personality, finances and careers of those who do their *living* there. It's the stage where the family acts out their roles and interact with one another.

The kanji for "southwest," the direction assigned for healthy relationships of all kinds.

"Do what you can, with what you have, where you can."
Theodore Roosevelt

Close this book now. Stop what you're doing, retreat to your hallway blindfolded and make an entrance into your living room. Now open your eyes. What grabs you? What was your childhood living room like? Can you get a picture?

In my mind's eye, the living room was the center of our suburban Michigan home. Double-glass sliding doors framed an all-season view of our swimming pool, comfortably surrounded by Dad's manicured, fenced in back yard. The clear, clean mirrorlike water was Tranquility City. Sometimes a little wind made waves. A natural Xanax. But the silence of this water world was totally shattered by the enormous large-screen color television, rarely turned off. The main attraction of our living room was the Motorola.

Every couch and chair was angled directly at the TV screen. This was our altar, and the La-Z-Boy loungers were our church pews. We never walked to church in our Sunday finery. Billy Graham came to our living room.

Anything that can be plugged into a wall socket like a computer, television, answering machine or blender has its own magnetic field. Mapping the human body, as recorded by the ancient Chinese acupuncturist's anatomical charts, involved measure and manipulation of magnetic fields centuries before Ben Franklin bottled lightning with his homemade kite and figured out how to make electricity believably visual. So it was with the Feng Shui masters who mapped magnetic fields of the human habitat: houses, mountains, valleys, ill winds, white water.

信
頼

The kanji for "confidence."

Feng Shui instructs us how to live within these overlapping 3-D magnetic fields by mastering their location. So don't let your cable installer take the easy way out. Tell him to put it where you want it. *You* know the whereabouts of your E Spot!

My Pop never heard of Feng Shui. (Normally, he wouldn't even touch chow mien.) But he did the right thing when he located our Motorola in the northeast corner. This was the "education" corner of our living room, Feng Shui tells us. So even though I got plugged into the racial memory bank with Lucy and Desi and the Cartwrights, loved school and when I brought home my report cards for paternal examination and approval, I was always at the top of my class.

"When you gaze long into the abyss, the abyss also gazes into you."
Nietzsche

The Form School of Feng Shui regards variations in landscape and terrain as vital influences.

Moira, a fellow Feng Shui enthusiast and astrologer from Chicago, has a son with movie star teeth, hair and buffed bod who was trying to break into show business. Throwing on her Adidas and leotard, she pushed the Sony TV into the southeast money corner of her living room and purposely tossed a soap opera magazine underneath a gold (the color of wealth) framed photo of her young stud muffin that sat on the TV. Days later he landed a cushy acting gig.

Where does *your* TV sit? What about the CD player, or answering machine? Every object like photos, collectibles, bric-a-brac that are in your constant line of vision sends off subliminal signals. Try me, use me, do me, be me.

For instance, a painting of an arid desert, particularly on a western wall, the sector dealing with children, may hamper your kid's motivations. On the other hand, hang a poster of fireworks there to suggest a willing readiness for things to start "popping." Or a beautiful ocean scene, synonymous to going with the flow to enhance perseverance and chutzpah.

Don't bombard yourself with icons recalling the way things used to be. Living rooms loaded with antiques or photos of dead relatives inhibit spontaneity and living in the moment. Relegate them to private spaces like bathrooms particularly if those belongings or people in the pix were prosperous and happy. Flea market treasures transmit subliminal messages to your space.

To prevent Excederin headaches and winter flu bugs, don't place statues or other heavy objects in the eastern health areas in your home, especially when sick or recovering. Instead, fill these spots with movement: mobiles, fountains, fish tanks, blinking Christmas lights to improve eating habits and reduce your Blue Cross premiums. Tear down all heavy metal music posters in the living room and replace them with green growing plants.

"East" (the kanji above) represents health, vitality and physical energy.

Demands for a level playing field have become buzzwords in political debate. But what we call "family values" can be inhibited and frustrated by a split-level playing field in home and household. There are family values in architecture, too, according to the ancient tenets of Feng Shui. But a sunken living room is not one of them.

If you're mortgaged with a multilevel ranch house or sunken living room and if you're looking for a possible cause of household hassles, family spats and moody recourse to the medicine cabinet, do what theatres do to avoid litigation. Outline every down step with tiny Christmas tree lights, illuminating from the ground up. This prevents spilled drinks, hip fractures and opens up opportunities for a harmonious household.

No less a champion of family values than Mae West, in her rare forays into the party circuit, travelled with a security guard at each elbow. Not to protect her from swooning fans or serial stalkers, but from suddenly sinking into Beverly Hills living rooms. Trying to wear wedgies and contact lenses at the same party can be daunting. And hip replacement surgeries have lost their mystique. Keep everything around the house on the level.

A living room's main energy spot is located at a diagonal from its main entrance and is called the power, or wealth, area. Keep this locale well-lit and clean. Prevent financial misfortune or getting suckered by scam artists by not using mirrors there. Use red or black-colored curtains and floral patterns to increase opportunity.

Aquariums and fast-growing plants (not cacti) can also be used here for increasing extra bucks, as long as you clean the fish tank regularly and trim all dead leaves from house plants. Replace all burnt-out light bulbs and belly-up dead fish ASAP to keep prosperity power surging.

On dry land, at least, most plants grow from the ground up between our toes or, like kudzu, behind our backs. But with the possible exception of the weeping willow, they rarely grow down from overhead. Hanging baskets of gorgeously tended plants may look inviting in fern bars and health food restaurants, but they can let loose vibes of restlessness and discomfort if they're dangling in the space above cash customers. Especially in an oasis of a family gathering place or living room. The rule is: no clutter anywhere near the power spot of your living room.

"The joy of life is to put out one's power in some natural and useful or harmless way. There is no other, and the real misery is not to do this."
Oliver W. Holmes

I had a very dramatic lesson in this area when I made a housecall on Diana who did heavy duty as a nurse in a big name Intensive Care Unit. Her job provided maximum stress. Migraine headaches were routine. But she had a green thumb and found gardening a favorite therapy for decompression.

When she led me into her living room, it was like an Amazonian jungle. Colorful exotic hanging plants filled the space over every seating area including her favorite chair in the northwest corner of her living room, the area that governs the head. She had become a full-time slave to her little green children. Wet-nursing them had become, she finally admitted, "a pain in the neck."

"Teachers open the door, but you must enter by yourself."
Chinese Proverb

I knew the remedy would be drastic, so I broke it to her gently. I told her about Ann Wigmore, the First Lithuanian Lady of Sprouts, who came to visit actress Gloria Swanson on tour in *Butterflies Are Free*. The concierge at the Ritz Carlton Hotel in Boston had received every floral tribute known to man for delivery to their star guest. But they hadn't reckoned with Ann, who was delivering two trays of buckwheat sprouts in raw salad length as an opening night tribute. Incredible but edible.

She knew Gloria wouldn't wear a flower in her hair (no corsage ever touched her shoulder) but carried a red carnation to inhibit the impulse for smoking. But as a woman who could afford the best of everything all her long life, she would prefer a salad of buckwheat sprouts to all the orchids on the Eastern seaboard.

So Diana re-potted and redesigned her Garden of Eden. She sprouts everything from lettuce and radish to alfalfa and mung beans. She created a new year-round garden: an indoor herb garden. Now all the plants are looking up, up and away. Headaches somehow disappeared along the way. Her colleagues, who now call themselves "health care providers" would, of course, call this spontaneous remission.

Physician, heal thyself. Or, better yet, try Feng Shui and heal your home!

"Problems, like babies, grow larger by nursing."
Ruth Holmes

Chapter Twelve
Home Cookin'

12

In addition to the bedroom, we spend a huge hunk of our life in the kitchen facing the refrigerator. The kitchen, Feng Shui says, is analogous to the liver: a place of cleansing, energy and support.

What do you loathe about your kitchen? Too few electrical outlets? Shelves cluttered with homework? Floors covered with shoes or boots? Is there ample storage space and cupboards? Do you use the kitchen for laundry, ironing, sewing? Is it your home office, too?

The kanji for "kitchen," one of the most important rooms in a home.

When I first moved into my home, the original yellow kitchen wallpaper was a claustrophobic nightmare. The oven range jutted out from the lower cabinets lining the walls, wounding unwary passersby. The giant refrigerator blocked the flow between table and sink disrupting, with its girth, the food prep area like a semi on a one-lane highway. And the window provided a bird's eye view of the neighbor's trash bin.

One of my first face-lifts meant blowing out walls to open up space, liposuction on the hanging green wall cabinets to enlarge the room plus an eye-lift: windows with better view. What changes did you make in your kitchen when you first moved in? Does it look like Momma's, Ivana's or Burger King's? Whatever, clean up the space. And keep it simple, organized and get rid of that junk drawer! Make it *yours.*

Hide all fondue pots and cheesy wedding presents; relegate china and pots and pans to an enclosed cabinet. While you're at it, recycle those ancient jars of supermarket herbs you brought from your old living space and replace them with fresh.

Keep everything within an arm's reach of the refrigerator, stove and sink...but, again, out of sight and away from your mind, not on display. To attract more personal time and curb the munchies, don't feature silverware or gadgets on shelves or hang pots and pans from the ceiling.

Before iceboxes, foodstuffs were stored in a ventilated cupboard beside the sink in what is called a larder — the best place for foods whose flavors diminish from refrigerated chill. Keep salt, flour, sugar, spices, pasta and condiments away from direct light in wooden, metal or dark glass containers to bring household security and happiness. Hang wire shelves or baskets for onions, apples and other perishables in a dark area beneath your work space to advance status as well as earnings.

北
東

"Northeast" represents higher thought, wisdom, understanding and knowledge. De-clutter and clean all northeast areas of every room when studying or perplexed.

Keep all food preparation areas spic and span. Consign leftovers and refuse to the compost pile to bring luck and happiness for your loved ones, or recycle them regularly for the homeless and hungry.

Freestanding refrigerators are okay as long as their doors don't interfere with food preparation or wandering, hungry guests. White, yellow or light blue are favorite fridge colors for curbing between meal snacking. Wood laminate is also good, although reddish hues stimulate salivation and increase late night pig outs.

Don't place magnets in the shapes of candy or food on the refrigerator door! Ditto for photos of yourself at your fattest. Instead, create a photo montage of your sveltest peers or display "skinny" pictures of yourself the way we were, and wannabe again alongside items that inspire you to eat healthy.

A chocaholic friend gave me some Hershey kitchen magnets shaped like candy bars for my first refrigerator. I've always been thin and my waist never enlarged. But within three months after hanging them on my fridge door, I gained ten pounds. Every time I saw them I got the urge for something to melt in my mouth (not in my hands). If you have a weight problem, retire all kitchen magnets that resemble candy, food or fat little pigs. And, unless you enjoy worrying about IRS tomorrows, refrain posting upcoming bills or overdue warnings on the icebox door.

A freestanding island or peninsula should be a good distance from the refrigerator for Feng Shui to flow in your kitchen. Heat cancels cold out. While improving my cooking area, the only available space for my toaster oven was atop the Westinghouse fridge. Bad move. The freezer iced up constantly and, weirdly, I had to replace my little oven twice within a few months, even though all appliances were brand new.

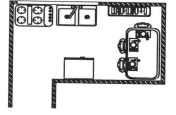

It's not good Feng Shui to place a stove (fire) next to a sink or dishwasher (water). Diners, as well as cooks, should be able to see who is coming or going both when seated or at the stove.

料理

The kanji for "cooking."

A freestanding oven island or peninsula unit doesn't isolate the cook from family or guests and provides a good visual scan of the room. If your stove is set in mid-kitchen and opposite the sink, husbands, wives and children will constantly argue. Built-in ovens flush to a wall work best allowing better traffic and ch'i flow. However, remember to use the mirror trick here because the baker's rear at the oven will moon the whole room.

Microchip technology and electro-sensor ceramic cooking surfaces are part of twenty-first century Feng Shui. Gas tops electric, natural versus nuclear, because it permits fine adjustments to the exact cooking temperature required and the heat halts the instant the burner is turned off. If you cook electric only or by microwave, decorate the area around the units with live, flowering plants or wooden artifacts (not too close!) to encourage foreign frequencies to attract better health for you and yours. Nothin' says lovin' like somethin' from the oven. Right?

Air and fume extractors come in an enormous variety. Many contemporary freestanding cook units feature extractor hoods over the burners, others hang suspended from the ceiling above or from a wall. With either style, it's important that they don't make loud noises that irritate the cook or detract from conversations. Kitchens featuring hanging fume extractors over island stove tops or preparation areas are definitely not propitious. (Remember Marie Antoinette.) No looming or shiny projectiles, please! Always keep fans as quiet and unobstrusive as possible. Don't think of them as objets d'art!

"Sometimes
I go about pitying
Myself,
While I am carried
By the wind
Across the sky."
  Ojibway Song

78

Keep your splashbacks (the wall area between your work top and hanging cabinets) sparkly clean. They should be made of durable material that can withstand water and scrubbing. Wood ones encourage family secrets as well as having a tendency to warp or attract insects. Shiny black ceramic tiles (the element of stability and physical growth) are excellent because they reflect the meal being created, symbolically doubling the food in the kitchen like a mirror and, hopefully, the money in your cookie jar. And, since time is money in capitalist lore, reflective tile surfaces also reduce scouring and cleaning energy, thus providing the gift of time.

Northern areas in rooms are concerned with career and work.

Sinks are essential in food preparation and often associated with tedious chores like washing up before and after. Because they are conductors and containers of water (the element of life and wealth), don't locate them too close to the stove or oven. Fire turns water to steam, not a compatible combo.

A stainless steel sink is your best choice for durability and reflective qualities, introducing the element of metal (symbolic of intuition and prosperity) into the kitchen. Enameled sinks crack and chip more easily than steel and are expensive to replace: a Feng Shui flaw inviting criticism, pettiness and laziness for the cook. Double sinks are preferred because two is the number of harmony and peace.

Keep cleaning products, dish cloths and sponges in a hidden but easily accessible area beneath the sink. To keep your family (and the cook) happy, don't let it turn into a catchall for cobwebs or expired cleaning products. Be sure to keep this spot organized and clean. Hang half-round carousels to get the most use from the dark depths of corner cupboards. Their constant flowing, circular motion will help keep things moving and increase cooperation between adults.

In many houses, rubbish is normally stored beneath the kitchen sink. Keep a lid on it. And consider putting a compost pile in your back yard or behind the garage to increase financial potential. When you recycle organic refuse back into your land, it's said that you'll always have money for necessary home repairs. To keep peace in your neighborhood, support your local recycling center with your empty bottles, cans and newspapers.

Pale yellows and blues are good Feng Shui colors for kitchen walls. Make sure the paint quality can endure constant washing and wiping. Whenever possible, use glossy paint for ceilings to reflect more light and bring your kitchen more energy. Wallpaper holds onto fumes and odors creating feelings of nostalgia and worries about the future and is not recommended.

"Follow your bliss. Find where it is and don't be afraid to follow it."
Joseph Campbell

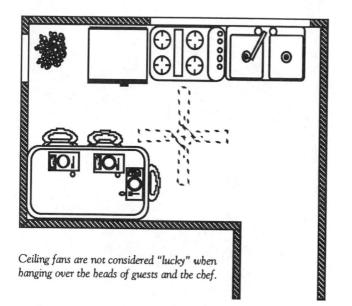

Ceiling fans are not considered "lucky" when hanging over the heads of guests and the chef.

Floors need to be tough enough to bear wear and tear from constant shuffling of feet and scraping chair legs and spilling and scuffing. Tile or flagstone beats linoleum for durability — either is better than carpet because they are more water-resistant and stronger. Polished wood floors are wonderful but require regular attention and resealing. To avoid family dissensions and financial pressure, never let a wooden floor tarnish or rot. Fix them up f-a-s-t!

敷
物

The kanji for "rug" and floors.

Synthetic rubber-tiled floors are great for spills and heat but thought to create superficial conversation, weariness. To increase warm exchanges between loved ones, place an odd number of different colored throw rugs on all such floors. Parquet coverings or checkerboard black and white patterns are out of place in home kitchens. They can create divisions and on-the-run-eating. Aim for unifying color schemes and simple patterns to encourage healthy family eating habits.

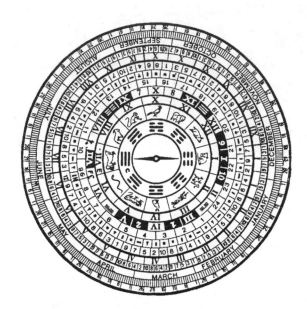

The lou-pan is the Feng Shui compass used to determine accurate directions and align a home to occupant's horoscopes.

Guidelines for master bedrooms:
• The shape of the room should not be irregular or have too many corners. Use mirrors, strategically place plants, fringe, electronic items, pictures.
• Round windows are not advisable, especially for single folks seeking relationships. If this is your case, hang a horizontal shelf below with live plants, photos of yourself at your happiest, most loved.
• The roof should not have a skylight above bed.
• It's not a good idea to have an aquarium in the master bedroom. Try fresh-cut flowers or silk ones.
• Japanese Feng Shui frowns on pictures and posters of water scenery; hang posters of sunrises, rainbows.

The bedroom door should not face:
• the toilet door. Keep it closed.
• the staircase or a corner.
• the door of another room.

The dresser should not:
• face another mirror.
• the door of your bedroom.
• be placed under a ceiling beam or post.
• be placed on both sides of your bed.

Chapter Thirteen
Home, Sweet, Sensual Home   *13*

Bedrooms are personal retreats where we spend about a third of our lifetimes (some, more than others, I'm sure). Whether we sleep on our side, our stomach or our back, bedrooms are largely places for horizontal rest, recovery, renewal. Dreary motel bedrooms, homes away from home, hotels or B & B's, we can't do much about. But with a room of our own for sleeping, waking, love-making or anything in-between, we can.

The two important words for a bedroom are "personal" and "retreat." According to British anthropologist Lord Raglan, bedrooms have gender (female). The connubial bed as a woman's turf with her husband as occasional guest is a custom dating from Old Testament times. Did you know the President of the United States sleeps in a peach bedroom with flying birds on the wallpaper? One of Pope John Paul I's acts as Supreme Pontiff was to send for his own favorite bed. His sudden death days later was attributed to its tardy arrival from Venice. ("Deathbed in Venice," anyone?)

According to the magical metaphors of Feng Shui, bedrooms are analogous to our breathing apparatus: our lungs. So, we should keep them clean, aired-out and avoid any kind of congestion.

The kanji for "bedroom." Invest time in assessing the color and the placement of furniture in your bedroom to increase personal happiness and luck.

Clutter invites dissatisfaction and conflict between bed partners. The color of your bedroom, position of the bed and decorative items play pivotal roles in either attracting or repelling good love and sex. A bedroom should be more square than rectangular to assure positive conjugal communication between couples, never triangular or featuring sunken or protruding corners.

Bedrooms are best at the back of the house away from the road, never above a garage, to increase happiness and sexual harmony. Sleeping rooms above garages increase insomnia, nightmares and crankiness. Light coming from either the right or left is good but do not expose bed sides directly to a window, especially in the rooms of infants and young children.

A bedroom should feel (and be) secure and intimate, never confining. Live or silk plants attract luck and happiness when visible from the bed. Remember to keep all plants pruned and healthy, remove all dead leaves. Yellow or pinkish flowering plants are best, contributing to individuality and personal strength.

You should never be able to see under the bed. If you can, cover it up so that it appears solid. Good Feng Shui beds are never more than two feet off the floor. The bed is the centerpiece of this room and, normally, the largest object of furniture. Which type is yours: a four-poster? Antique? Futon? Trolley or trundle? Sofa bed?

It's preferable to have beds close enough to the floor or to have bedspreads long enough to hide what's beneath. Fear and apprehension over future

"Whoever you are, no matter how lonely,
the world offers itself to your imagination,
calls to you like the wild geese,
harsh and exciting —
over and over announcing your place in the family of things."
Mary Oliver

projects become magnified whenever the space below a bed is visible. Try shams, dangle sheets. Lower the mattress. To encourage a good night's rest, never sleep atop storage boxes, books or things hidden under the bed. Keep textbooks, magazines, radios, clocks and televisions several arm lengths away from your pillow. Otherwise, dreams will be frantic. Nothing, including trailing ivy, lamps or skylights, should intrude in the space above your bed. So take down the ceiling mirrors and hock your trapeze.

I vividly remember Mr. Jameson, my freshman college journalism professor, telling us to sleep with crib notes next to our noggins the night before a final exam. I tried it. Sure enough, I had dreams of active verbs and bylines all night long. And, I aced the test! I still repeat this ritual whenever I have an upcoming speaking date or a TV spot. I highly recommend it. Give it a try.

The kanji of "love."

Futons and foam mattresses are favorite Feng Shui bed choices, although best with ventilated bases, not solid. Always flip and air them out regularly. Open- and pocketed-spring mattresses are better for adults rather than children or seniors, inviting a good snooze and sense of self.

Keep all joints on sofa or trundle beds well-oiled to encourage sweet dreams and peace of mind. Enhance longevity and family harmony by frequently recycling mattresses and box springs. To increase productivity and opportunity, buy new sheets and pillowcases every few months. We tune up the car regularly for good mileage; why not regularly realign your sleeping quarters?

"I arise today
Through the strength of heaven,
Light of sun,
Radiance of moon,
Splendor of fire,
Speed of lightning,
Swiftness of wind,
Depth of sea,
Stability of earth,
Firmness of rock."
Saint Patrick

Cynthia's charismatic minister-husband divorced her four years ago after twenty-three years of marriage, but she still had great difficulty considering herself "single." Her claustrophobic bedroom walls were adorned with "he and she" photos and she still slept on the same ivory silk sheets they shared as newlyweds. Only after repainting the room, burning the old linens and buying new bed coverings could she finally sing O Solo, Mio. Controlling her space and buying new sheets gave her the confidence to be her own person. She's single still, but far more comfortable with the dating game than ever before.

Traditional Feng Shui insists that the karmic energies (what goes around, comes around) of people live in objects and gifts from others. It's said that when sleeping on an inherited antique bed, the joys and hardships of those who used it before will affect you now, so make sure that the provenance includes someone you can admire. Invest in new bed coverings and change your life. Where you snooze, is where you can lose, too. So beware, and be aware!

"Zen Buddhists say that a finger is needed to point to the moon, but that we should not trouble ourselves with the finger once the moon is recognized."
Fritjof Capra

The colors of a room, the positioning of the bed, the arrangement and decor, play pivotal roles in enhancing sweet dreams and sweet couplings or disenchantment that begins between the sheets. Take a deep breath and look around.

In the twenties, when Chinoiserie, an oriental equivalent of European haute couture, began to make its way into U.S. pictorial magazines and movies, one of the high priestesses of chic was

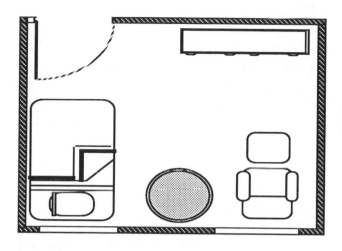

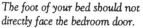

The foot of your bed should not directly face the bedroom door.

British romance novelist Elinor Glynn. She was decades ahead of Martha Stewart at telling women what to do by doing it, conspicuously, first. Madame Glynn never travelled without her own sheets, pillows, drapes and rugs. She refused to risk spending any dream time in other people's home threads and furnishings. She would sooner wear secondhand clothes. Luxurious ocean liner and train travel made her whims possible.

West is the direction concerned with offspring, stepchildren and pets.

Unless you have your own Lear jet, or a lover's yacht, you can't always imitate Madame G. But at home, you can dictate the shape and color of your sleeping quarters with the ruthlessness of a bedouin prince or oriental princess.

If you are brave wannabe parents and your Blue Cross card doesn't cover all the protracted trials at the fertility clinic, try repainting your master bedroom a lively shade of green. Let the sun shine in on arrangements of flowering plants on the floor near the bed. Green is the color of seedlings, sprouts and new growth and it brings to mind the wonder of renewal, life.

The psychic connection between green and new life means it's an ideal color for a nursery or the private room for your first newborn. Feng Shui masters assign specific values to the colors of the rainbow. Different shades for different maids. Blue rooms turn occupants into the opposite of what blue means in the west. Sky color suggests relief from stress. Irving Berlin wrote about smiling blue skies. Restful repose and sweet dreaming.

Yellow, the color of sunshine, evokes invitation, social and intellectual interchange. It is great for libraries, studies and family rumpus rooms and terrific for adult bedrooms.

"Strike me pink," "in the pink," evokes a color of revival, happiness, love. Carrie Fisher titled her second book *Surrendering The Pink*. Pink is the color of intimate body orifices. The Chinese masters recommend this shade as ideal for reviving failing romances. Think about it.

"What is the color of wind?"
Zen Koan

Blue bedrooms relieve stress and prompt good rest. *The Red and the Black*, the classic French novel by Stendahl, made into a great film starring Gerard Phillipe, helps us to remember that those two shades most often appropriated by the ecclesiastical monsignors and cardinals, reek of hierarchy, paternalism and intimidation. These are colors of inequality, S & M, black leather and red blood. When striving for equality in a union, avoid red or black bedrooms. If anyone you meet has a boudoir in these shades, put your shoes back on and run for your life!

To enhance good health and communication among loved ones, do not locate ceiling fans over the bed, only off to the side. Ditto for placing a bed under a sloping ceiling or exposed beam. If this is your fix, move either the bed or fan and paint overhead beams the same color as the ceiling to promote fidelity and honest dialogue.

Sarah and Joe, a professional couple in their twenties, were unsuccessful at starting a family until they moved their waterbed away from the overhead ceiling fan. Joe likened this cooling swirling guillotine to a butcher's electric meat cutter, slicing away at him while he slept, making intimacy impossible. To add insult to infertility, their bedroom was triangular with several sharp corners. Not good for heir conditioning or intimate coupling.

Beware of rectangular bedrooms, including trailer homes, mini-vans without built-in bidets. Equality in human relationships is enhanced by bedrooms that have equal length sides, his and hers, parity. In a room where all sides are equal, you probably won't need to visit the X-rated section at the local Blockbuster outlet.

"Of all sad words of tongue or pen, The saddest are these: It might have been."
John G. Whittier

To avoid bad dreams and poor finances, don't sleep with your feet aimed to the bathroom door, or a toilet, bidet or sink basin. If this is your case, either always keep the bathroom door closed or hang a full-length mirror facing the bed to counteract disappointment.

Make sure you always have a full view of your bedroom door in order to see who's entering. Keep digital alarm clocks and television sets at least six to nine feet away from where your head rests for a good night's sleep and inspired sweet dreams.

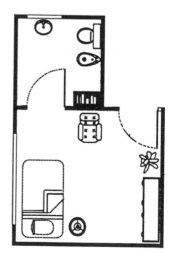

Canopied beds with rounded posts and anchored ruffles are built for seclusion, isolation, chocolate stains on marabou feathers. Beds you don't want to get out of. All alone on the telephone. Nothing, including hanging plants, lamps or skylights, should be above the bed so get rid of that mirrored ceiling!

Sometimes these picturesque mini-tent cities are antiques, real or fake. Circular beds make for short-lived relationships (*Playboy*'s Hugh Hefner's favorite shape bed before fatherhood).

Sleeping on an antique bed invites entangling yourself in all the karma of the inferno of fornication and the tumult of previous sleepers. Get rid of it. If the four poster can't be auctioned off at Sotheby's, order a new mattress. And take down the overhead ruffles. When moving to a new home or apartment, buy a new bed and mattress. If the budget is shaky, leave the old mattress behind or buy new sheets and linen.

"The worst loneliness is not to be comfortable with yourself."
Mark Twain

It's not good Feng Shui to have a mirror at the foot of the bed whether freestanding or above a bureau. And never ever hang mirrors that are broken, cracked or damaged either. This not only interferes with your sleep, it also ensures a rude awakening and a slap in the face, seeing yourself warts and all as you rise and try to shine.

To enhance good health and sex, don't sleep beneath a skylight or window or let your bed face a toilet. Keep the toilet seat down and lock the door! To prevent insomnia and attract prosperity and martial bliss, remove all mirrors, aquariums or pictures of watery scenery from above the headboard. Similarly, the back of your headboard should not be placed in front of a window.

Round windows in a bedroom are not favorably regarded in Feng Shui, although circular or oval mirrors on side walls are OK. Square windows and mirrors, the shape of awareness in the real world, are best. Doors should not face a staircase, mirror, long hallway, corner or door of another room. If this is your situation, place tall plants, stone statues or hang a wind chime from the ceiling at strategic spots to divert the eye.

Windows to the world, like windows to the soul, are often more provocative and interesting if they are heavily veiled. Remember? Window dressings, curtains and lighting are important. Windows should feature curtains or blinds that are not opaque and easily controlled. Table lamps on a nearby nightstand rather than overhead lights give you more control.

"The race is not always to the swift, but to those who keep on running."
English Proverb

Track lighting is good for highlighting paintings or art objects. However, his and her twin light switches should be controlled independently from either side of the bed. Overhead lighting is for surgery, pimple-popping and Diana and Charles.

To increase self-esteem and a good night's sleep, let a bed rest against a wall but never a mirrored wall or window. For peaceful sleep, don't place a mirror so it is directly at the foot of the bed or have a television nearby. Whether at home or the Hyatt, never doze with the TV on. Place the TV at least nine feet away from your pillow. Ditto for the radio or CD player and VCR.

Alarm clocks, especially digital electric models, should keep their distance at least six feet away from pillows, rousting you out of bed rather than allowing you to press the snooze control and begin the day kvetching. Remove or dismantle shelves on walls near the head of the bed.

To avoid insecurity and paranoia, don't sleep with your feet directly facing a doorway. Beds should be catty-corner to the door to allow you to see who's coming or going. Hang wind chimes either in entrance ways or by windows to enhance good sleep and vitality.

"Bless the moment, trust yourself and expect the best."
Hunan Philosophy

Burn sweet-smelling incense or candles, like vanilla, apple, cinnamon or frankincense to promote happy dreams and family unity.

Like Charles Dickens, many believe that facing east while lying in bed brings happiness and health to family members and guarantees fidelity. To attract a mate, face southwest. Turn your bed to face southeast or north to attract wealth and business opportunities, south for fame and recognition for future generations. If rearranging the placement of your bed is impossible, place live, lush green plants in the direction of the energy you want to attract.

In the bedroom, wall closets or walk-ins are always better than freestanding wardrobe bureaus. Decorate all chests or armoires with ivy or live green plants and photos of children or favorite vacation spots to promote growth in personal affairs. Avoid health problems by never placing such objects at the foot of a bed. Relegate photos of ancestors or old flames to the den.

Bedrooms for the old folks should be bright with windows but be sure that sunshine or moonlight doesn't fall on the bed. To increase life and alertness, refrain from using cut flowers or plastic flora. Only live, breathing green, please. Decorate the sleeping rooms of loved ones with current photographs only and decorate in shades of off-white, yellow, salmon or gold-ish-beige. Older loved one's bedrooms are best away from gathering and living rooms but with easy access to a bathroom to insure integrity and independence.

Never rush off to the office without looking back over your shoulder. Have you left behind an unmade, rumpled mess? Making your bed might magically make your day.

Home Security
Bedrooms For Your Babies

As kids, we quickly learned that certain rules are different for grown-ups. In Feng Shui, the same is true for bedrooms of the young and their parents. Until puberty, rectangular or square rooms are better than odd shapes. Locating a child's room near or behind the kitchen or in the center of the home is not wise. Avoid wild stuffed animals and sharp, swordlike objects for decor.

Curious little hands love to peel and peek beneath wallpaper. Paint all surfaces in lead-free washable paint. Yellow is the color of mental stimulation and the favorite for a youngster's bedroom. Light green or blue shades provide relaxation and assist in a good night's sleep and, hopefully, inhibit nightmares and sugar rushes.

Placing the bed in the north helps develop intuition; in the northeast, a child's experimentive skills will shine. Sleep and downtime go better with beds in the eastern sector. The southeast inspires perseverance in work and an awareness of future economic concerns; in the south, good reputation and awareness of status quo. A healthy awareness about love is accented with beds set in the southwest; a southern placed mattress emphasizes good health and eating habits; in the northwest, help from friends and coworkers.

Premium floor space is a must for young games, homework and wrestling. Teens do better with throw rugs than pre-teens. Until then, carpeting (berber versus shag) is better than linoleum or wood. Floor coverings need regular cleaning, and worn-out carpeting needs immediate repair to help prevent the youngsters from being insecure or becoming "stuck" in their learning.

"We've had bad luck with our kids— they've all grown up."
Christopher Morley

Older children don't usually appreciate sharing rooms with siblings. Freestanding screens that separate beds and desks will subconsciously urge youngsters to be their own person. It's not a good idea for a little one to sleep beneath a skylight, especially if they are prone to nightmares or bed-wetting.

Bunk beds are space-savers but not recommended. Humans sleep best when close to the ground, not stacked like the Holiday Inn Attica. If your child sleeps in a lower bunk, cover the underside of the top bed with a light yellow or green fabric to make the little one more confident, less dependent on approval from others.

Up until adolescence, use wall-mounted lights rather than desktop or table models to give them control in their waking hours. A wall lamp that can be turned off and on comfortably near the head of the child's bed inspires security and prompts reading. Pinwheels on shelves or colorful spinning mobiles in the shape of fish or planets hung from the ceiling can stimulate ideas and mental competition. Lazy or slow students will find that napping on dark green or yellow pillowcases is good for test-taking.

Sleeping on a firm but lightweight washable foam mattress will incite a child's interests and curiosity. Stay away from hard, firm types. Fitted sheets help prevent feelings of insecurity and restless sleep. Avoid busy cartoon patterns and go for solids. To curb insomnia, do not store toys or clothes beneath children's beds or too close to their resting heads. And keep their beds away from overhead ceiling beams and fans. To provide awareness of who they are, don't hang posters or pictures over their pillows.

Hang a mobile of fish or place an aquarium in the northeast area of a child's bedroom to stimulate curiousity and encourage academic competition.

Don't create a "theme" in your children's bedrooms — let them personalize *their* way. A recent study by psychologists analyzed the dorm rooms of college freshmen. Frosh who decorated their rooms with snapshots, *Playboy* centerfolds, campus maps, astrology charts, or pictures of sunsets dropped out less than those who left the walls bare. Personalizing a room is everything.

Chapter Fourteen
14 *Home Entertainment*

Feng Shui's founding fathers didn't do McDonald's. Back then, daily meals were shared with family and "I love you" meant "I will cook for you," not "Do you want fries with that?" Rooms used exclusively for dining were a feature of royal palaces, unusual in the West among the commoners until the late eighteenth century. Until then, tables were set up in any convenient spot, or bowls were balanced in laps and meals were taken wherever and whenever.

Growing up absurd in the 1950s, I remember more TV dinners in front of the boob tube than sit-down suppers which is probably why I'm an entertainment and TV junkie.

"If your eyes are blinded with your worries, you cannot see the beauty of the sunset."
Krishnamurti

In Feng Shui, the dining room is analogous to the spleen and nothing should divert attention from food or conversation. It is best for a dining room not to be visible from the front entrance; try to make it a special, separate part of your home. Unlike glass-walled fast food places overlooking parking lots or speeding traffic nudging you to hit the road, a few windows help promote concentration, amusing conversation, and serious chewing instead of eat and run.

It's preferable not to see the kitchen from the dining room. If these rooms are too close, stand a screen between them or hang a crystal chandelier above the table or a small crystal ball from the ceiling to distract the eye and separate the space symbolically. To prevent arguments and promote intestinal peace when Domino's delivers, set out silverware and serve in the dining room, not on the couch with a napkin in your lap.

Highlight the food on the table, not the cooking and serving area. If your freestanding dining table is connected to the kitchen, learn from Orson Welles. Use foreground spot lights and dimmers to make background clutter disappear into the shadows, creating a more seductive and appetizing illusion of space. Hide refuse and dirty pots and pans, never flaunt them.

To further avoid digestive and cultural misunderstandings, never place the table facing a staircase or toilet. If space constraints make repositioning impossible, locate tall live plants in the appropriate line of vision. If the table seats guests under a ceiling beam, move it, or paint the beam to match the ceiling to ward off irritability and anxiety.

To increase companionship and intimacy, don't put dining room tables below drainage pipes that run in the ceiling or below a toilet. If this is your situation, hang a chandelier above the table and let the CDs play on.

For dining rooms, pale walls are best. Low tones promote a relaxing mood, complement food and guests and look great by day as well as candlelight. Pale green and yellow stimulate lively conversation; grays and beige make for neutral shop talk. Formal dining rooms reserved exclusively for evening should feature light rose tones to enhance pleasant exchanges among guests

"When we refuse air, light and food, the body suffers. And when we turn away from meditation and prayer, we likewise deprive our minds, our emotions and our intuitions of vitally needed support. As the body can fail its purpose for lack of nourishment, so can the soul."
Alcoholics Anonymous

while providing an attractive background for silver, glassware, wedding gifts and gilded bric-a-brac. Bright red dining rooms are for restaurants that encourage patrons to eat and run. Chez vous? Never!

Comfortable chairs are a must! Good food is ruined when your butt hurts or chairs are too tight or squeaky. Aim for comfort and elbow room as well as eye contact. Let the kids eat on the floor if they want. Adults need the secure personal feel, and space, of a sturdy chair.

"My tidiness and my untidiness are full of regret and remorse and complex feelings."
Natalia Ginsberg

"We rarely have dinner guests," Sherry, a Chicago TV producer, warned me as we sat down for supper recently in her contemporary suburban brownstone. I immediately understood why. The "food table," as she called it, was piled high with work assignments and kids' homework, as well as being bathed in bright fluorescent lights that exaggerated every pore and blemish. To make matters worse, her table was inches away from the stove, sink and trash compactor. Not a pretty sight or good for sound diffusion.

We sat in antique cast-iron chairs that made my Calvins and me uncomfortable. The heat from the oven, the chef's sweaty brow and grinding noises from the kitchen were distracting and irritating. A bird's eye view of the onion skins, potato peelings and tomato "blood" on fancy grey formica cabinets resembled a designer garbage pail. Martha Stewart would have had a coronary!

When eating in groups, visual contact and table traffic-flow is important. Low-hanging pendant lights, chandeliers or ill-placed candelabras can block eye contact or interfere with passing appetizers. If you cannot see the guest with whom you're talking, it's tough to understand their point of view. Wall sconces and dimmer switches provide ambient, non-invasive light and help curb disagreements.

Skylights above the dining room table are fine provided they are not directly overhead. Use light-colored tablecloths, not busy Laura Ashley-type patterns that tend to confound the eye. Try to keep it simple.

Place honored guests in chairs that face the main doorway, the power spot, and not where they see food prepared. Let the chef sit closest to the cooking area; close kitchen doors. But during the day, keep dining room entrances open to invite energy into your home, to help air circulate and attract health and prosperity for the hungry.

The kanji for "food."

When eating, lower dining room curtains, especially when the view is unappetizing or competes with the cuisine. To ease digestion, willowy, soft curtains are preferred over louvre blinds or shades. Here, softness creates a feeling of comfort and relaxation, inviting you to sit back and enjoy the food instead of playing peek-a-boo. Don't seat anyone with their back to a window until the curtains are drawn unless it's an in-law you despise or a colleague who's a pain.

Be sure the table is solid not rickety, warped or soiled. Glass-top tables impel guests to leave early, featuring feet and prompting escapist strategies. The ideal Feng Shui dining table is preferably oval, octagonal, round, rectangular or square,

"Blessed is the spot, and the house, and the place, and the city, and the heart, and the mountain, and the refuge, and the cave, and the valley, and the land, and the sea, and the island..."
Baha'i Prayer

in that order. Wood is better than laminate or glass. Keep it simply decorated, light and airy, and with live or silk flowers in-between feasts.

Hide all tableware and glasses in sideboards, cabinets or dressers. Don't distract from a meal by displaying bric-a-brac on walls or shelves. In a dining room, the attraction is the food and *then* the "look" of the table. Not your great-grandma's napkin rings.

Walls should feature mirrors (to detect parsley between your pearly whites or egg on your face). Paintings of landscapes and nature attract luck, money and cut down visits to the doctor. To prevent discord and confusion, don't display liquor bottles or photos of grandpa in the dining room. Keep unused china and crystal out of sight. Otherwise, everyone will want seconds and thirds and might lose touch with the purpose of the gathering. This is especially important for households with children.

"*Anger as soon is fed is dead*
'Tis starving makes it fat."
Emily Dickinson

Wood, rather than linoleum or tile, is the preferred Feng Shui floor covering. Light-colored, like silver birch, is better than dark. Throw rugs work better than wall-to-wall carpeting and help avoid spills and wear and tear from chair movement. Pastel colored carpets are preferred because they reflect light from windows or skylights and, according to Feng Shui tenets, bring serenity and peace among diners.

Make sure your kitchen nook has plenty of elbow room. This is a private, cooling-down spot for folks in a hurry. They need "breathing space" until their morning caffeine kicks in. Lighting should

come from the sides rather than above; windows
are best. Wall sconces are next best, sending
light to the heavens while at the same time
illuminating the food below. Ditch all dramatic
objets d'art, mobiles or items that might distract
you from business at hand. Calm entertaining
pictures and food posters or plants on the table
work best; nothing too dramatic or heavy.

Empty plates and happy faces tell us we are truly,
deeply, madly loved.

I will cook for you.
I will eat your food.

Think food, not furnishings.

"My world turns and goes
back to the place
Where, a thousand forgotten
years ago,
The bird and the blowing wind
Were like me, and were
my brothers."
    Herman Hesse

101

Chapter Fifteen
15 Home Necessities

The grounding of our modern mania for cleanliness was laid, sociologists say, in century sixteen through eighteen. Aggrandizing monarchs formed court societies with highly demanding standards of personal parfum. For the upwardly mobile, cleanliness was the key to nobility. The French buzzword "noblesse oblige" meant, among other things, that the sweet smell of sweat was reserved for the privacy of the boudoir.

Japanese culture, like early urban American, used public baths. The Ellis Island showers could accommodate 8,000 tired and poor wretches a day. The triumph of cleanliness came after World War II when houses with plumbed bathtubs became available to most working class Americans, save the very poor. The pursuit of clean brought hot water and stall showers inside, fringe benefits of civilization few would care to give up.

America's high standards of clean surely contribute to disease control, real and imaginary. What the diseasestablishment euphemizes as "health care" begins in the bathroom with flossing, brushing and scrubbing and other elements of personal hygiene that have not yet been taken over by the credentialed Ph.D., M.D. classes.

"I believe in the sun even when it doesn't shine; I believe in love even when it is not shown; I believe in God even when She doesn't speak."
M. Walker

The Chinese word *shui* — water, the element of life, prosperity — is also their slang word for money. Today, the bathroom, or water closet, is a private refuge for cleansing the body, inside and out. One of the most important rooms in a home. Color it in passive, light colors with water-resistant paint, keep it uncluttered and have adequate lighting, curtained windows and good ventilation. The lavatory is concerned with your personal health and wealth.

When I moved into my home, the original upstairs master bathroom had only enough space for a small sink, toilet and a pygmy size tub. There was no room for maneuvering or storing dirty towels and underwear. One of my first reconstruction jobs was to expand this area by blowing out a bedroom next door and the attic above, creating a tall cathedral ceiling. It's now as spacious as a private chapel and no one leaves the loo in a hurry. And, to date, no one living in my home has ever used their Blue Cross card or bounced a check.

The kanji for "bathroom" looks like a septic tank beneath a home.

Properly lit bathrooms are a must. Recessed lights are good for shower and tub areas; wall-mounted surface lights are best for shaving, washing and tooth-brushing spots. Above the basins, extra light on the front and sides of mirrors is recommended, helping you to be more aware of your potentials as well as shortcomings. Diffused light is better than fluorescent; natural light is best.

Remove window panes and replace them with mirrors cut to size that fill the entire area to create more privacy and the illusion of more space. Trade in clear glass windows for opaque frosted glass or hang a stained glass art object over them to bring peace of mind and relaxation.

A proper Feng Shui bathroom allows you to sit comfortably on a porcelain throne without facing a mirror (everyone deserves privacy in the privy). The best spot for the toilet is far away from the door to allow the ch'i and household energy to circulate comfortably and not get flushed away. Hang a long mirror behind or on top of the toilet, or place a small plant or cut flowers nearby in a black container with several small round-shape rocks if the loo is too close to the door.

Poor bathroom locations are the center of a home, above a front entrance way or next to the kitchen. The toilet is called "the Devil's Room" in several Eastern cultures. If your lavatory is centrally located, hang large floor-length mirrors on both sides of the door, add a wind chime or pipe in music for privacy. Mirrors will not only make guests feel more comfortable, but they are like a doorbell and will also prompt others to knock before entering.

Bathrooms visible from either a kitchen, dining or bedroom will erode individuality and personal belief. To bring success to future projects, leave the bathroom door slightly ajar when unoccupied.

To insure a sense of calmness, the toilet should be out of sight. A screen, room divider or curtain between it and the entry way acts as a shield, energizing the room and stimulating ch'i (and your guests) to meander. If size limitations prevent this, always remember to keep the toilet lid closed.

Does your toilet or bidet sit on the floor? Or is it hung from the wall? Receptacles that sit securely on the floor are preferred in Feng Shui. Wall-hung ones multiply floor space filth, dust,

"Think of your own faults the first part of the night when you are awake, and of the faults of others the latter part of the night when you are asleep."
Chinese Proverb

unwelcome cobwebs. For wall-mounted seats, place a red or black colored throw rug beneath to encourage good sanitary habits and attract wealth.

Make sure all flushing mechanisms are quiet and function well. No noise or leaks, please. Replace cracked or fading cushioned toilet seats immediately. To enhance dignity and a sense of purpose, keep toilet paper within arm's reach, not hidden in fancy camouflaged spots!

"Like water which can clearly mirror the sky and the trees only so long as its surface is undisturbed, the mind can only reflect the true image of Self when it is tranquil and wholly relaxed."
Indra Devi

Pedestal sinks have a central support system which normally conceals plumbing and is better Feng Shui than wall-hung basins. Areas beneath wall-hung units often become catchall, makeshift towel or rag racks and may interfere with your ability to hang onto money. This also applies to bath tubs: floor-sitting ones are better than claw footed, freestanding.

Double or triple basins are better than single: the more areas that produce water, the more opportunity for prosperity and investment diversity. Oval basins are better than square or rectangular ones, for they send subliminal signals to relax, take your time.

Mirrors should be large enough to reflect your entire body. Small mirrors that cut you off at the knee inhibit vitality and curb open mindedness. Polish all mirrors regularly and immediately replace burnt-out bathroom light bulbs to promote vitality. To maintain balance with the elements, rectangular or square mirrors (governed by earth, a healthy complement to water) are better than pointed, triangular ones (fire counteracts water) in the water closet.

It's preferable not to use wall-to-wall carpeting in bathrooms; ceramic tile (earth) is the floor covering of choice. For wood floors, place small, thick area rugs generously in high traffic spots.

Although light pastel blue, green and ivory are good for walls, rich slate, deep greens and dark blues are best for floors. Floor tiles can be cold in the winter and slippery when wet. Warmth is essential but electricity and water don't mix, so keep radiators and built-in wall heaters away from wet hands.

To inhibit drains on your finances, immediately repair all leaking faucets and toilets, otherwise it's as if you're throwing money down the drain; plus the irritating drip-drip noises interrupt concentration. To insure self-worth and confidence, remove all makeup, cosmetics, extra toothbrushes or shampoo bottles from counter tops.

"They must often change who would be constant in happiness and wisdom."
Confucius

Conceal waste pipes, drains or overflows and hide all toilet brushes, cleaning products and utensils to enhance economic growth and in-home happiness.

"Coming clean" requires admitting our errors. To be "all washed up" is to be out of the swim. "Taking a bath" can mean financial disaster. So grab the scouring power, close the bathroom door and come clean!

Chapter Sixteen
Home Base

With the right kind of accident insurance, you can make love anywhere in the house from the shower stall to the kitchen sink. But what does your compass say about where you sleep? Where is the bed located? On which side do you rest? What about your regular partner or guests when they sleep over? Is your sofa convertible? Where do you unfold the futon?

Dig out the blueprints of your home sweet home. Do certain corners protrude? Have certain improvements sliced away at the symmetry of your domestic rectangle?

方位

The kanji for "direction."

Modern floor plans are designed for looks, cost, comfort and approval by the commissars of your local building permit office, who decree how much concrete is kosher for a driveway or three car garage. Modern Feng Shui takes site plans into another dimension where you consciously consider the trees, sun and shade, water, and vibes of a neighborhood, as well as chemical assaults on surrounding lawns, rather than what the building inspector says. Man-made madness versus God's Green Acre.

Over the centuries, Feng Shui has evolved into splinter groups. The Compass School, one of its oldest and more arcane branches, aligns personal space in accord with precise compass directions and historical as well as metaphysical lore.

Each direction has a different impact on each person. For instance, here in the Mid-west, driving east in morning rush hour requires sunglasses plus clever maneuvering of your car's sun visor in order to see properly. Not when heading west.

Most Feng Shui schools use an eight-sided chart called a ba-gua (pronounced *bah-gwah*) to discover the strengths and weaknesses of living spaces. It resembles an octagonal pizza cut into eight slices. Each piece of the ba-gua has specific traits that influence the actual compass direction of your home or work place.

The ba-gua's directions and influences are:

- *South* social standing, status and acknowledgment from peers;
- *Southeast* finances and savings;
- *East* health and your parental family;
- *North* job, career and work
- *Northeast* education, credentials;
- *Northwest* your support system and luck while travelling;
- *West* children, plants and pets;
- *Southwest* personal and love relationships.

Home Plate
Using The Ba-Gua

To assess the ch'i "power spots" of a space, run to a hobby or auto store and buy yourself a compass. Take off your wrist watch and bracelets and stand about four feet in front of your original main entrance door and face the street outside. The direction your nose points to is the compass direction of your home. Ch'i energy, it's said, enters from the original and main front door, no matter where you usually sneak in: from the side, back porch or garage.

• Then, take the compass direction of your building's front door remembering that true north means true north, south equals south, and so on. Next, walk through each room and either tape small file cards or stick 'em notes with the actual compass direction on every wall.

"Step out onto the planet.
Draw a circle a hundred feet round.

Inside the circle are 300 things
nobody understands, and, maybe
nobody's ever really seen.

How many can you find?"
  Lew Welch

• Make a photocopy of the ba-gua on page 111 and "stretch" it over your floor plan like wall-to-wall carpeting.

• Next, superimpose your compass-aligned ba-gua in every room, noting which walls and corners face east, south and so on. If your marriage or money sectors appear to be in inauspicious places, don't fret.

• Finally, walk room-to room and write the ba-gua keywords associated with each direction on your file cards or stick 'em notes.

Is your favorite easy chair placed in the west? (Don't you worry *enough* about the kids? Move it to the northwest corner for stress-free travel and more recreation time.) Does your kitchen fall in the eastern health sector? Good! This promotes healthier eating habits.

• One final word about the ba-gua: don't get hung-up on minutiae! Feng Shui endeavors to restore harmony within your walls. For every "curse," there's a "cure."

Traditional Feng Shui philosophy says that every room has specific impacts when walls or corners protrude or are indented.

The kanji for "recognition," governed by the south.

Northern protruding walls or corners are unfavorable. Hollow north spots set you up for an accident-prone household. Decorate these areas with floor-to-ceiling mirrors, hang trailing live green plants over the offending spots, or paint them in red or yellow tones. Protrusions here can create rebellious, egocentric and reckless kids, while adults may suffer ongoing kidney or urinary problems. Folk lore suggests that grown-ups who don't use good Feng Shui judgment risk the needs of their offspring.

In the northeast, protruding areas stimulate resident's minds but may aggravate the stomach and digestion. Sons will not easily accept defeat. Aim all floor or desk lamps into these spots or install your stereo or CD player here.

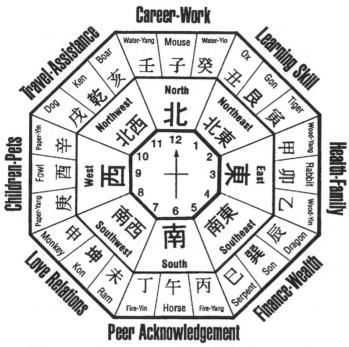

Superimpose the ba-gua over the floorplan of each room aligning it to the actual compass direction of every wall and corner.

Hang trophies of family achievements in the northeast sector for good communication and continued united family support.

Hollow eastern areas bring difficult balancing acts for family life and career with the potential for liver problems, poor eating habits. In this situation, family members may suffer low self-esteem, discouragement from peers, and frequent financial hassles. Protrusions in the east can increase risk-taking and impatience.

Stacy, a young single-mom auto exec, was thrilled about moving into her new suburban home. She loved its locale and spacious new bedroom. Unfortunately, her twelve year old's room resembled a crushed milk carton: a jumble of seven jagged walls instead of four, each jutting in or out in various angles and depth. Waking up in her perfectly symmetrical northern career area of her new digs, she prospered and enjoyed life.

"Must it be?
It must be."
Beethoven

111

"We never know how high we are
till we are called to rise."
Emily Dickinson

Meanwhile, son Greg's grades and health declined after just weeks of sleeping in his convoluted carnival fun house-shaped eastern quarters. When he was diagnosed with hepatitis, Stacy moved him to the smooth, four-walled guest room in the west, for children's well-being. Greg quickly recovered from liver disorder, became the happiest guest in the house and honor roll student, and president of his seventh grade class.

Women and daughters who sleep in bedrooms with southeast indentations are asking for heartbreak and sad love affairs according to Feng Shui history. Place an aquarium with an odd number of red fish and one black in this area to deny any galling tears.

Families with protruding southeastern bedrooms or living areas will need to exert much effort to succeed. Keep all southeastern spots that jut outwards clean, and constantly move or hang photos of family or pictures of tall mountains or trees to bring romantic as well as financial happiness.

Southern protrusions are said to enhance adult reputations, especially women's, when in the southwest areas of a home. Southern rooms with indented corners attract dangerous friends and consequent heart problems for ladies; southwest hollow spots make for lazy husbands and abdominal stress for all involved. Here is the place for table fans, wedding presents and anniversary photos of you and your spouse or old lovers in your happier times.

Protruding western walls are said to promise a happy family life. But beware! Daughters may develop respiratory or problematic asthma as well as a tendency to be flirtatious when there are hollow or "missing" spots here. Paint these areas in dark shades of green, hang deep emerald fringed wall coverings. Or place wedding photos to attract family security and good communication.

In northwest corners, hollow or protruding areas can create ongoing quarrels, competition among loved ones and potential respiratory problems for fathers or husbands. Hang a bird cage or painting of a mountain range or seascape here for objectivity and help from others.

Sam, my secretary's father-in-law, an Italian in his late fifties, kept his bed situated in a sunken northwest corner with sloping ceiling overhead for over twenty years. He struggled with emphysema from his daily two pack cigarette habit. Moving his bed to the squared-off, bright east side of the room seemed to make it easier to overcome his smoking addiction and defy the deadly prognosis. He even took up jogging and horseback riding: the northwest's emphasis for exercise, travel and movement!

"Good actions are the invisible hinges on the doors of heaven."
Victor Hugo

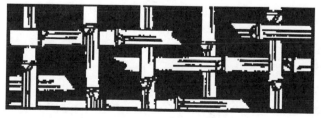

Chapter Seventeen
17 *Home Offices*

There's a special ba-gua for your office desk, too. Go pull up a chair, take a seat at your work station or bill-paying table.

Is the chair wobbly? Fix or replace it and attract financial gain. Is the area clean and clear, or does it look like a Malibu mudslide? A messy desk "creates" disturbance; organized environments beget happiness.

The area opposite your seat (regardless of the direction you face) is called the fame section. This top, center spot symbolizes how others see you, your willingness to succeed and grow in addition to respectful acknowledgment from peers and coworkers.

The area to its right concerns your personal relationships and unions of love. Just below and to the right deals with children: adopted, step- and grand-babies as well as pets. Luck and good fortune when travelling and kindness of strangers along the way is the area where your right elbow rests. Where your belly rubs is the area of career and hobbies.

The upper left desk corner is the money section denoting your capacity to earn and save. Just below is health and physical vitality. The area where your left elbow rests concerns knowledge, education, government agencies, lawyers and how

"Though we travel the world over to find the beautiful, we must carry it with us or we find it not."

Ralph Waldo Emerson

you learn. When rearranging desktops, always affirm what it is that you desire; intention means everything when rearranging. Intone your purpose as Asians do.

Feng Shui employs many symbolic objects that "power up" what you find lacking in your life. For instance, light-reflecting objects like leaded crystals, shiny picture frames or mirrors open doors of opportunity. Living things such as flowers, plants (real or silk, no cacti or plastic plants, please) and aquariums invite growth. Bells and wind chimes represent communication and act as magnets to enhance your power.

Electric items like TVs, lights, computers or CD and tape recorders invite power and strength as do moving mobiles. Heavy props like statues or rocks add stability in shaky circumstances.

Each desk area is assigned a particular color. Green evokes growth, red for energy, white for intuition and awareness, black with power and money and yellow or gold for intellect. Try it!

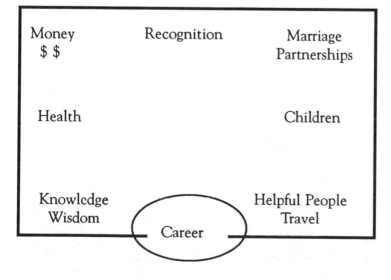

My mother in Florida recently telephoned in a panic after receiving a telegram that my brother was lost somewhere in the Pacific Islands. After placing his picture and three brass bells in the children section of her desk plus a box of bandages and aspirin (for safety) in the travel portion, she received a telephone call assuring her of his arrival within days. Unfortunately, she also placed a cactus in the money section and he returned flat broke (cacti deal with slow growth, stagnation).

Another Bloomfield Hills mama was constantly harassed at work with pleas of help and handouts from her kids. She moved the telephone from the children section of her office desk and her offspring somehow got the message and grew up.

To attract prosperity, pile business checks on a small octagonal mirror in the money section of your desk or a drawer in that locale. Wise writers keep the word processor or pens and pencils there too. Marketing moguls and salespersons should constantly activate the power network for helpful people and fame portion of the desk with business cards in order to increase contacts and productivity. Japanese tycoons travel with Gucci leather trophy baggage displaying business cards of their rich and famous CEOs.

"Every man has a rainy corner in his life, from which bad weather besets him."
Jean Paul Richter

Each sector of a desk top governs a certain body organ (see below). For instance, as your next checkup with the behavioral optometrist nears, activate the area across from your chair with a red or green tchatchke; for sinuses or hay fever therapy accent the right elbow region of the desk with something blue and pleasant to look at; for the urologist or OB-GYN, place pink quartz or another pinkish object in the upper-right of the desk. Remember to visualize and affirm what you desire whenever activating an area.

De-clutter your desk and your life.
Change your fate—redecorate!

作業場

The kanji for "work space."

• *Sit at your desk. Regardless of the direction you face, this area directly in front of you deals with career, what you want to be when you "grow up" and job aspirations. Activate it with black objects (stones, etc.) or with dark onyx gems. This area governs the ears.*
• *The area directly in front of you deals with how others perceive you, fame and recognition, and governs the eyes. Activate it with red-colored objects, or tiger's eye gems.*
• *The spot in the front, top left of your desk deals with money-making and prosperity, and the colors red, blue or purple. It governs your hips and upper thighs. Ruby and red beryl are its precious gems.*
• *The front, top right-hand side of the desk is concerned with personal relationships, marriage and love commitments, in addition to the health of the reproductive/sexual organs. Its gem is pink quartz and pink tourmaline and is activated by white, pink or red-colored objects.*
• *The area at your left elbow deals with your hands and your ability to learn and comprehend. Activate it with dark green, black and deep blue-colored objects, or the gems blue angelite or blue sapphire.*
• *The spot where your right elbow rests is concerned with travel and people who will help you get what you need. Diamonds or clear quartz are its favorite gems, and the colors black, grey and white. This quadrant deals with migraines and the head.*
• *The area between this and the upper-right section of the desk is concerned with children, pets and favorite houseplants, as well as your teeth, lips and mouth. Embellish it with white objects or pearls.*
• *The area across from it, the middle left-part of the desk, governs your feet and ankles and overall health of you and your loved ones. Activate it with green-colored objects or emeralds.*

18 Chapter Eighteen
Home Alone

An eminent media critic once described my radio talkshow as "despair therapy." The intimacy of the telephone prompted more lucid tell-alls, he felt, than *Oprah*'s TV hot seat. For every confessor who got through, there were scores waiting on hold forced to listen to other people's troubles. He attributed Motown's shrinking suicide rate to my three hours of DT on Sunday night.

For those who couldn't get through on the phone lines, there was the post office. Some of my mail came from people who did not have cellular phones in their prison cells. Prompted by an on-air discussion of the impact places have on people, a guy named Steve with several numbers after his name wrote to me from the Jackson Reformatory about reforming his habitat according to the tenets of Feng Shui.

It was the ultimate challenge; a sharp reminder of the cultural chasm that divides us taxpayers from the million-plus men and women who inhabit the world's largest gulag archipelago.

Here is a synopsis of our exchange:
• In the good old days before his arrest for marketing drugs without a license, Steve had a regular cleaning lady to keep his deluxe digs bright and shiny. He was now punishing himself, he admitted, by leaving his metal wash basin a mess, crusted with toothpaste, hair and spit.

"More dangers have deceived men than forced them."
Francis Bacon

After I explained how scouring is empowering, he disinfected his entire space and, as directed, found proper places for color pictures of rainbows, flowers and transcontinental jets like the Concorde on the drab windowless walls of his cell. Within weeks, his letters began to lighten up. He was relaxed, clear and began to trust and confide in me.

• He followed through on my idea of finding a way to place a screen around his open toilet, which dominated the space. The warden would have nothing to do with it. He nixed windchimes. There was no way Steve would be allowed to mount an electric water pump to turn his toilet into a mini-Trevi fountain, let alone placing one by his sliding cell door: a harbinger of prosperity.

But he did get away with placing a nightstand in his southeast corner with a picture of Niagara Falls. The table had eight sides prompting financial gain and the union of spirit with body and on it he put a red place mat and digital clock. Soon, he had a choice job working in the prison kitchen.

"God gives us the nuts, but He doesn't crack them."
German Proverb

• One of the fringe benefits of his new gig was the gift of life: potato peelings, radish and carrot tops, dried beans and lentils and grains. All these live foods would live on and he sprouted them in tin cans mounted on his wash stand. He sent me sketches of what now looked like a miniature green Eden. Trailing vines on three sides. However, the warden drew the line at having hardy English ivy crawling along prison bars. Never mind. His abode was now crawling with live energy. Ch'i.

Metal frames without glass contained pictures of rolling hills and landscapes turned bare walls into trompe l'oeil windows. Soon his letters were whooping with joy because his insomnia had withered away. Nightmares vanished. So he began adding and refining.

• After placing a poster of exploding fireworks in the north corner, for career, he began graduate studies in architecture. He built a small bookcase decorated with dimes and quarters beneath the poster and started an in-house Feng Shui "consulting business" which brought extra pretzel and telephone money.

• Days after hanging in his northwest wall, the area for obtaining assistance from others, a Hallmark card of a businessman on the telephone, Steve's lawyer was on the horn with news of a transfer to a minimum security facility. A new flower and on-site assessment Feng Shui business quickly followed together with the promise of parole.

"The reason angels can fly is that they take themselves so lightly."
G. K. Chesterton

Ghandi brought the British Empire to heel from a prison cell by doing a fast. From Thoreau to Mandela, we learn again that spiritual development can thrive amid the most awesome injustice.

Change what you can change.

Chapter Nineteen
Homing In On Business

Modern day property developers discover that floors number 4 or 9 are unpopular on the Pacific Rim. The number 4 and the Japanese word for "death" sound the same. Similarly, the number 9 sounds like "pain" and can turn a penthouse into a death house. Many businesses in that part of the world take drastic measures to avoid numbers that include or add up to the number 4.

The new Hong Kong Marriott Hotel recently hired a Feng Shui consultant who advised placing a ceramic horse with its head turned up, the symbol of endurance and strength over competitors, in the marketing director's office and moving the cash registers. After the geomancer's tips, occupancy level became the highest on Hong Kong Island.

"The more you know the less you understand."
Tao Te Ching

Not to be outdone, the Hyatt Regency Singapore aligned their main entrance doors to stand at a 35-degree angle. Soon more guests beat a path to them.

When a Feng Shui master was flown down to Sydney, Australia, to inspect the Hyatt Kingsgate, they complained their piano bar was a disaster area. The reason the bar was doing poorly, he said, was that patrons had a panoramic view of the toilet and all its two-way traffic. He suggested they block that view. After installing a large, opaque glass screen, happy hours and bloated bar tabs rattled the registers.

The Feng Shui master was horrified to discover the funneling effect of the escalators between the ground floor and reception area. It's not advantageous to have a staircase or escalator descending directly towards an entranceway. Think of energy "running" away to escape like rain during a downpour. Being greeted by a down escalator makes profits and patrons run away.

Next, he moved the sales director's desk to face east (money) and all confidential file cabinets were trundled away from a facing doorway to prevent their secrets from "flying away" on this runway. After these and other changes, occupancies at the Hyatt jumped by 11 percent. Marketing Director John Wallis said, "the overnight changes were uncanny, to put it mildly." After returning to his Chicago headquarters, Wallis quickly moved his desk to face east towards a window.

Other firms with properties in Asia, including the new Hong Kong Ritz Carlton, use Feng Shui consultants to determine auspicious dates for ceremonial openings. On this side of the world, real estate tycoon Donald Trump proudly acknowledges he has several Feng Shui practitioners on his payroll in order to one-up his competitors.

Don't sit with your back to a door or window with strong sunlight. You will be outlined as a silhouette and not as a whole person, suggesting incompetence. One Feng Shui safety measure is to keep your desk chair at least three feet from the wall. Otherwise, you weaken your power position if too close. For career security, place a rock or statue in the northern portion of the office.

"Work is love made visible. And if you cannot work with love but only with distaste, it is better that you should leave your work and sit at the gate of the temple and take alms from those who work for joy."
Kahlil Gibran

No windows in your work space or favorite lounging area? Life-giving ch'i energy won't circulate or stay, repelling opportunity and happiness. Wave a hand-held fan like Karl Lagerfeld (to keep things moving), fill your place with live or silk flowers (inviting growth), toss a few shiny metal (like coins, for prosperity) pencil containers on your desk. Best of all, natural or full-spectrum illumination versus fluorescent lights assures productivity and mental well-being. Dark spaces are unhappy, unhealthy. Fill your space with light and life. Trust your instincts, follow your intuition.

The kanji for "money."

Look at those photos of White House interiors. You never saw FDR with his jaunty cigarette fencing with the press against a background of White House windows. Those high windows in the Oval Office were a favorite posing ground for JFK and Bobby. Particularly during the Bay of Pigs' disaster.

Our president should beware of Kennedy imitations. He could use some distance between his Oval Office desk and the rear windows. To attract, project and deliver authority, he needs some solid backing in the East Room. Now that we've avoided a trade war with China, maybe our First Lady should elevate the Presidential Seal to the space atop the Presidential rear windows? The First Couple got where they are against all odds. This might help him not just to reign but to lead.

Mom always nagged us to keep our rooms clean. Feng Shui agrees and takes it a step further: When there's harmony in your personal space, there will be order in your own little universe.

Chapter Twenty
20 *Home Sick*

We are what we think we are (a TV anchor personality, heavyweight champion, rock star, First Lady) until that telephone rings and it whisks you back to reality.

The next voice you hear may be a recorded message informing you that you are next...of kin. And all a.k.a. assumed identities dissolve as we become sons, daughters, mamas, papas, cousins to cousins, nieces and nephews. Someone you love doesn't want to be a burden. But the insurance has run out, and they wanna send 'em home. For survivors, sudden death is often easier to handle than the alternative.

"When you dig another out of trouble, you find a place to bury your own."
Cathy Teal

If any experience can compel you to appreciate some humble abode, it's a few days (daze) in the hospital. But home alone waiting by the telephone for Ms. HMO Godot, the visiting nurse, can be stressful enough to send you back to intensive care. The only surefire remedy is l-o-v-e. Do unto someone the way someone may some day (you hope) do unto you.

Voltaire described the art of medicine as entertainment of the patient while Nature does the healing. And, when it comes to entertaining recovering loved ones, Feng Shui provides lots to learn and make do. And remember, you don't need a license from the city or a Ph.D. in anything to move furniture, hang drapes, make soup, edit CDs, rent home care necessities, massage extremities or, even, wipe butts.

Gretchen, an attractive Munich matron in her mid-sixties, enjoyed her jet-set life whisking around the world painting flattering portraits of the rich and famous. Her work adorned the walls of corporate palaces and country club collections. An active artist-on-the-run, she was also a diabetic. She ignored her doctor's orders to have cataracts in both eyes removed until she could barely see. Frightened by the thought of going blind, Gretchen finally consented to an operation.

The day before being discharged she phoned local visiting nurses and her shrink from her hospital bed. Then, she placed one to me for Feng Shui physical therapy.

How do you create a Feng Shui "healing room?"

Many sick people are often tucked away in a bedroom far from the mainstream of the house. Sometimes, isolation is necessary. But for Gretchen, still mentally alert behind her designer sunglasses, it would have been disastrous, depriving her of family comings and goings, the telephone, music and the opportunity to feel a part of daily domestic life. In most cases, to be able to hear and see everything that goes on contributes to one's sense of living a normal life.

For Gretchen, I relocated her chaise lounge to the northeast, the sector for knowledge, self-help and understanding, which had a lovely, unobstructed view to the east (the spot concerned with a family's well-being) where the sun also rises. Sittings and paintings could resume in natural, not fluorescent lighting.

"Although the world is full of suffering, it is also full of the overcoming of it."
Helen Keller

Gretchen's operations were successful and she bewildered her doctors with her rapid recovery. Currently, she's in Taiwan doing another portrait and thirty minutes daily of ta'i ch'i exercises. Her hotel room, filled with flowers and mementoes of loved ones, faces a lovely western garden (the direction of health). Her bed is located in the west, as well.

Choose a room, or rooms, that are most comfortable and convenient. Are they in the activity mainstream and still in a space where other family members may have visitors, play and work? Can you hear someone call from that room?

Does your loved one like to be alone (if so, place the bed in the south, great for discovering tips about one's individual worth), or is their couch in the northwest (which would make them yearn for outside stimulation and a little help from friends)?

Whenever possible, arrange a separate room for the patient to sleep in at night (preferably in a northeast corner like Gretchen's), and another nook for daytime activities, visiting, and being with loved ones. Try the east or southeast sectors to encourage family participation.

Would resting in the living room (an important Feng Shui domain) be a better choice? Trade places in your imagination with the sick person. At home, a person is special, not a room number. In a hospital, you learn how disturbing it is to have impersonal traffic traipsing in and out.

Sunlight nourishes the body and soul. Pick a room with windows open to the outside world: the sky, trees or next door neighbors. Freestanding screens and draperies can provide plenty of privacy and are good Feng Shui remedies for many ills. Let Ma Nature do her thing.

Will they be spending lots of time in the bedroom? If so, activate the east and western corners with music, mobiles, aquariums. Will they be running a business from the bedside? Move them to a southeast or northern spot.

Do they love TV, the tabloids or music? Again, energize the northeast. Are they depressed or moping? Try accenting the south area with freshly cut plants, new books, cards from friends. Feng Shui says keep things within reach to increase alertness and zest for life.

The "convalescing room" kanji.

Change the furniture arrangement for patients who need a walker or wheelchair. Remove all scatter rugs to prevent tripping and activate their northwest sector with electrical devices like TV or computers to encourage mobility and self confidence. Rearrange all furniture to make easy access to a bathroom, hallway or dining room, and explore ways to enlarge their space. There are many remedies worse than a patient's disorders. "Home" is where the heart is. Make it so.

For good Feng Shui, locate a patient's bed catty-corner to the doorway with easy access from both sides. This makes turning, moving and changing sheets easier. Put futons in storage and beware of mattresses too close to a floor. On the same account, soft, sloping elevated mattresses can suddenly give away and provoke tumbles.

Bedside tables on both sides to encourage stretching, eye and head movement as well as personal ch'i is the place for drinking glasses (drinking from metal or heavy ceramic ones is said to increase confidence), straws, medications, cosmetics, a small hand mirror, cassette player or radio, and tissues.

Provide plenty of warm socks or nonskid slippers within easy reach. A stand-up bed tray allows leisurely dining and is good Feng Shui. Small tables with a vaporizer on each side of the bed are a must for patients with respiratory problems, especially during winter when heat dries the air. Take time to grab the massage oil and rub-a-dub-dub. Think about what you would like done to *your* body and do unto others.

Communication with the outside world can be enormously healing. An extension telephone cord, a cordless on the nightstand with a turnoff bell in the northwest or northern corner of their bedtable or a small hand-held bell or buzzer is super-smart and may promote the healing process.

Keep all potty chairs or bedpans under the bed, out of sight but handy. Use floor or desk fans to circulate ch'i and provide good ventilation. Keep spaces smelling fresh. If you become nauseous while playing nurse, put perfume under your nose and breathe through your mouth. One day you might be trading places.

Bathrooms are the most perilous places in a home, so they need special consideration. Too many are tiny, cramped, and difficult to move around in. Provide easily accessible lighting and keep sanitary needs within an arm's reach from

the toilet. Remove all throw rugs. A wobbly person on the potty should be able to reach the sink and tub without having to stretch, lean or dangerously strain. If sitting or getting up presents problems, try elevated seats or railings to overcome the difficulties. Shop the local hospital supply outlet and keep the telephone number of your Feng Shui practitioner handy.

"There's always room for improvement — it's the biggest room in every home!"
Hazel Dawkins

Ideally, ailing loved ones should be able to see the bathroom door (the place for health and regeneration) from their bed, so make sure there is a night light and ample illumination.

Keep the bathroom door cracked open when not in use, never fully closed and make sure the door opens and closes easily. Is the floor slippery or tiled? If so, install temporary rubber floor coverings in shades of green or yellow to promote quick recovery and mental alertness. Make sure all routes to the toilet, tub or shower and other bathroom units are free and safe, no matter how small. Relocate anything that can slip or be tripped over. Remove floor hampers or place them against the walls, and store all cleaning utensils out of sight.

Hide any clutter that's on the bathroom sink, especially those with a wide counter top. Sink top chaos impedes healing and invites spills. Bathroom faucet spots enhance longevity and good health, so make sure they function properly. Temporarily replace faucet handles with large styles for anyone with hand or arm injuries to speed up healing, add more comfort and encourage their independence.

"No great thing is created suddenly."
Epictetus

Activate the north area (dealing with eyes, arms and hands) to assist in a fast recovery as I did in Gretchen's home. Use solid-toned towels in Feng Shui's healing tones of violet, blues or greens instead of heavy striped or busy patterns to increase stamina.

What delights *your* schnozzola when you're sick? Flowers, incense, perfume, freshly laundered sheets? Feng Shui research reveals that a hint of vanilla or cinnamon and apple cider in a vaporizer or atomizer spray in the northeast corner during sleep time makes for sweet dreams and heightened appetite. Ask your patient and work it out.

A Parisian in the play *The Madwoman of Chaillot* adored garbage as "the smell of God's plenty." Aroma-appreciation is more developed in some noses than others. For centuries, aromatic oils have been part of religion and healing.

Many fragrant essential oils are antibacterial as well as antiseptic, helping to prevent the spread of germs and viruses. Chinese country hospitals still burn rosemary and lavender in their corridors to cleanse "bad vibes" and to prevent nightmares.

Orange blossoms and rinds, chamomile and marjoram may cause the brain to release a seductive and sedative neurochemical that is calming and relaxing, says Feng Shui. Fragrances like basil, lemon or peppermint stimulate memory and mental alertness. Experiment with spearmint just for the smell of it! Call your local aromatherapist or herbalist for tips.

"We have no right to ask, when sorrow comes, Why did this happen to me? unless we ask the same question for every joy that comes our way."
P. S. Bernstein

Among other things, try raiding the rainbow for Feng Shui "remedies." Do your market-testing. Peachy pink toned walls and sheets are said to help those who suffer from depression. Greens and azure blues are also calming.

Orchids, lavenders and purples bring you in tune with your spiritual nature. Many relate deep green, browns, greys and dark reds to depression, so anyone smitten with dread disorders should steer clear of them. To the sick, these colors smack of pessimism and fear. Try bright yellows like the color of the sun to counteract feelings of remorse.

Repaint the walls or pamper your patient with solid tone sheets and pillows to spark their recovery. Go ask them for *their* favorite shades and indulge them.

What kind of music should fill their room? Pleasant sounds like classical or Gregorian chanteuse can soothe the spirit and heal the cells. Japanese and Eastern Indian masters believe the flute speaks to the soul. Allow your baby to "control" surrounding sounds. Present choices, and make them comfortable with the mechanics of all sound-making devices. Or place a feeder outside bedroom windows to attract groups of birds and ch'i which is better than the sound of a doctor's beeper or clanging hospital trays!

Adorn rooms with plants, whether live or silk, but beware of certain live greens which may breed germs like those with curly, scalloped leaves that collect dust; they are best kept away from postoperative patients. Small aquariums with odd numbers of black and red fish, a small cage for birds or family pets contribute to the sense of life in a recovery room. Alternate wall hangings and rotate cut flowers and potted plants.

For rapid recovery, continue to immerse loved ones in life, life and more life.

Homerooms for Convalescing Kids

In a child's room, activity and companionship are vital in most cases. In addition to basic supplies, move baskets of comic books, magazines, toys conveniently near the bed or in the northeast or western corners to stimulate learning and self-entertainment. Every child has a treasured toy or doll which can be prominently displayed to remind them of happier days. Let your ailing young one make their own "Do Not Disturb" or "Do Not Vacuum" sign for their door.

The kanji "west," the direction designated for children.

Indian Feng Shui masters urge you to keep a blackboard near a child's bed to encourage mental exercise, especially for kids recovering from throat or tonsil troubles. A hanging mobile (especially in the west or east parts of a ceiling) delights the eyes and generates healthy ch'i. Keep televisions and digital alarm clocks at least six feet from the headboard of youngsters' beds to prevent nocturnal overstimulation and bad dreams. Instead, empower them with a remote control or binoculars.

Patterns of home care depend on the condition and needs of a patient, capacities of friends and on your credit rating. Healthy Feng Shui demands conscious choices and constant movement.

It's all about "wind and water" — elements that are both steadfast yet changing.

Chapter Twenty-One
21   *Home Free*

Experiment with the following Feng Shui ceremonies every birthday to attract year-round success and happiness.

Kanji for "human life."

• To help keep promises to yourself, hang a brass wind chime above your desk or on the back door of your main entrance. Brass insures clarity of your dreams; glass or aluminum chimes bring quick, swift luck but nothing long lasting.

• To overcome relationship and career challenges successfully, unblock doorways and remove items stored behind all doors. Cluttered, busy doorways are like having a stuffed nose, promoting an out of sort feeling and desire to sleep. On the same account, to attract new friends and business leads hide snow boots and winter paraphernalia from sight of entrances.

• To bring career options and successful acquaintances into your life, greet one new person every day for twenty-seven days, but do not make demands, requests or complaints.

• Moving or rearranging at least twenty-seven things in your living space every twenty-nine days attracts opportunities for better money making and open-mindedness. Try it today!

• For peace of mind and body, avoid being in direct line with the door and place your bed and desk so you can easily see the entrance. Sit at a desk that is spacious and clean, allowing room for the expansion of your ideas. Always keep your desk uncluttered and organized.

• For insight and the cultivation of good luck, place books and live flowers where you see them as you enter your space.

Kanji for "daily life."

• To make every birthday one of recognition and to welcome improved status, sing every morning, noon and evening: in the bathroom, the shower and the car.

• To attract prosperity, mirror the area behind your kitchen stove, reflecting and doubling the burners. Your cooking symbolizes wealth. The more burners, the larger your income. If mirrors are impossible in this crowded space, use shiny silver plates or place new dimes, quarters or silver dollars, even aluminum foil.

• If your dining room has only three walls, place a screen to create one more. If not, jittery conversation and the need to escape will prevail. To attract health and happiness for those living in your space, rid the eating area of business papers, cook books or utensils, knic knacs and mess.

- Make sure you have no leaky faucets in your home, especially in the bathroom! Dripping, leaking water diminishes your capacity to save and plan for the future.

- To invite opportunity and support from others, check out your front door. Paint it, unsqueak the hinges, make sure all locks and doorknobs function properly.

- If the views from your windows are unattractive, hide them! If it's not possible to hang curtains, put a bowl of goldfish (an odd number, please) on a table near the offending window. And make a point during the next twelve months never to sit with your back to a door or window.

- To add compassion and love to your relationships, hang a round mirror in your bedroom. Keep all electrical or digital equipment at least ten to fifteen feet from your head and leave all old magazines or comic books in a shrouded, unseen area or closet.

> *Sow a thought and you reap an act;*
> *Sow an act and you reap a habit;*
> *Sow a habit and you reap a character;*
> *Sow a character and you reap a destiny.*
> Ralph Waldo Emerson

Suggested Reading & Bibliography

Campbell, Joseph, *The Mythic Image*. Princeton
   University Press, 1974
Ching, Francis, *Architecture: Form, Space and Order*.
   New York: Van Norstrand, 1979
Day, Christopher, *Places of the Soul*. Aquarian, 1990
Eitel, Ernest, *Feng Shui*. Synergetic Press, 1984
Finster, Elaine Jay, *Health, Wealth, and Balance
   Through Feng Shui*. 1995
Gallagher, Winifred, *The Power of Place*. New York,
   Simon and Schuster, 1993
Govert, Johndennis, *Feng Shui: Art and Harmony of
   Place*. Daikakuji Publications, 1993
Jung, Carl, *Man and his Symbols*. Princeton, 1975
Hiss, Tony, *The Experience of Place*. Knoftof, 1990
Jacobs, Jane, *The Death and Life of Great American
   Cities*. Random House, 1961
Itoh, Teiji, *The Gardens of Japan*. Kodansha
   International, 1984
Kostof, Spiro, *The Architect*. Oxford U Press, 1985
Lawlor, Robert, *Sacred Geometry*. Crossroads, 1982
Lim, Jami, *Earth Design*. Earth Design, 1995
Lip, Evelyn, *Feng Shui for the Home*. Heian, 1990
Longacre, Bob, *Sweet Fern magazine*. Self-Pub, 1995
Mann, A.T., *Sacred Architecture*. Element, 1993
Marfori, Mark, *Feng Shui: Discover Money, Health
   and Love*. Dragon Publishing, 1993
O'Brien, Joanne, *The Elements of Feng Shui*.
   Great Britain, Element Books, 1991
Pennick, Nigel, *The Ancient Science of Geomancy*.
   Thames & Hudson, 1979
Rossbach, Sarah, *Feng Shui: The Chinese Art of
   Placement*. E. P. Dutton, 1983
Rybczynski, *The Most Beautiful House in the World*
   Penguin Books, 1990
Spear, William, *Feng Shui Made Easy*. HarperCollins
Swan, James A., *The Power of Place*. Quest, 1991
Thompson, Angel, *Feng Shui: Creating Balance and
   Harmony Through Design & Placement*. St. Martins
Walters, Derek, *The Feng Shui Handbook*. London,
   The Aquarian Press, 1991
Wilhelm, Richard (trans.), *The I-Ching*. Princeton
Williams, C., *Outlines of Chinese Symbolism*. Dover
Wydra, Nancilee, *Feng Shui: Designing Your Future:
   A Contemporary Look at Feng Shui*. Heian, 1995

Index

A

aborigine 2
address 2, 12, 15, 21, 24
aluminum 52, 134, 135
apartment 2, 6, 15, 21, 90
aquarium 52, 72, 90, 112, 115, 127, 132
aroma 38, 131
astrology 3, 5, 95

B

ba-gua 109, 110, 114
back alley 15
Bali 6
basement 7, 9, 15, 53, 58
bathroom
    5, 47, 51, 60, 61, 71, 93, 102, 103,
    104, 105, 106, 127, 128, 129, 130,
    135, 136
bathtub 102
beams 89, 95, 97
bed
    3, 5, 13, 17, 22, 23, 24, 36, 37, 38,
    39, 41, 49, 51, 60, 61, 63, 64, 65,
    66, 75, 84, 85, 86, 87, 88, 89, 90,
    91, 92, 93, 94, 95, 96, 103, 105,
    106, 110, 114, 115, 116, 120, 126,
    127, 128, 129, 130, 131, 132, 135,
    136, 137
beige 22, 47, 93, 97
Bermuda Triangle 6
bidets 10, 89
black
    21, 22, 41, 42, 45, 46, 58, 72, 79, 81,
    86, 88, 104, 105, 112, 115, 132, 133
Black Hat Sect 10
blue
    22, 36, 37, 38, 47, 56, 76, 87, 88,
    93, 103, 106, 117
bonsai tree 5
brown 22, 40, 98, 132
Buddha 32

C

cabinet
    53, 71, 75, 76, 79, 98, 100, 122
carpet
    27, 28, 48, 81, 94, 100, 106, 109
CD player 55, 70, 91, 110
ceiling
    3, 11, 23, 52, 61, 64, 76, 78, 80,
    85, 89, 90, 91, 95, 96, 97, 103,
    110, 113, 133
chairs
    9, 68, 73, 81, 98, 99, 100, 110, 114,
    117, 122, 127, 128
ch'i
    7, 8, 15, 18, 20, 23, 24, 28, 35,
    78, 104, 109, 123, 126, 128, 132, 133
China 14, 22, 34, 56, 123
Chinese
    2, 3, 12, 31, 47, 68, 88, 102, 131
circle 18, 19, 50, 53, 65, 80, 91
closet
    5, 24, 92, 102, 105, 136
clutter 29, 72, 75, 97, 130
color
    2, 3, 8, 15, 20, 21, 22, 23, 27, 28, 39,
    45, 46, 47, 48, 49, 51, 60, 64, 66,
    67, 68, 70, 81, 84, 87, 88, 89, 93,
    103, 115, 119, 132
columns 22, 23
communication
    27, 28, 41, 43, 84, 89, 111, 113, 115
compass
    10, 107, 108, 109
Compass School 10, 107
compost 31, 35, 38, 76, 80
computer 12, 31, 68, 115, 127
curtains
    3, 5, 9, 59, 64, 66, 72, 91, 99, 136

> *"When you meet a master swordsman,*
> *show him your sword.*
> *When you meet a man who*
> *is not a poet,*
> *do not show him your poem."*
> Lin-Chi

About the Author

Dennis Fairchild is born under the Chinese Year of the Metal Tiger — the oriental sign of quick wits, enthusiasm, original thinking and determination.

A writer, world traveller and international lecturer, Fairchild left Michigan State University to be a globe-trotting actor-astrologer for the rock musical *Hair* in the 1970s before settling in Birmingham, Michigan. His interest in Feng Shui and metaphysics earned him kudos as host of "the longest-running prime time 'ask the astrologer' talkradio show in Michigan's history of broadcasting."

Kanji of "helpful people."

He has appeared as an on-going guest on National Public Radio, CNN, the Tonight Show starring Johnny Carson, the Sally Jessy-Raphael Show, and is the ABC-TV Special News' titleholder as "Detroit's most accurate psychic."

For information on Fairchild's seminars, tapes and books, please write or telephone:

Dennis Fairchild
c/o WaveField Books
Post Office Box 1781
Birmingham MI 48012-1781
tel: 810. 646.3555
fax: 810. 646.0711
e-mail: HealHome@aol.com